Evangelical
Interpretation

Evangelical Interpretation

Perspectives on Hermeneutical Issues

Millard J. Erickson

Baker Books

A Division of Baker Book House Co.
Grand Rapids, Michigan 49516

Published by Baker Books
a division of Baker Book House Company
P. O. Box 6287, Grand Rapids, Michigan 49516-6287

Printed in the United States of America

Library of Congress Cataloging-in-Publication Data

Erickson, Millard J.
    Evangelical interpretation : perspectives on hermeneutical issues /
Millard J. Erickson.
      p. cm.
    Includes indexes.
    ISBN 0–8010–3220–2
    1. Bible—hermeneutics. 2. Evangelicalism. I. Title.
BS476.E653   1993
220.6′01—dc20   93–14903

To John and Beverly Englund

Dedicated Christians and Faithful Friends

Contents

Preface 9

1. The Nature of Authorial Intent 11
2. The Role of the Holy Spirit in Biblical Interpretation 33
3. Getting from There to Here: *The Problem of Contemporization of the Biblical Message* 55
4. The Contributions of Church History, Theology, and Cross-Cultural Studies to the Hermeneutical Task 77
5. A New Paradigm? *Postmodernism and Hermeneutics* 99

Scripture Index 127
Subject Index 129

Preface

A decade ago, a great deal of attention was given to the question of the truth of the Bible, or inerrancy, as it is termed. More recently, attention has turned to the hermeneutical task, or the issue of the Bible's meaning. The issues of hermeneutics that are currently in the forefront are not, however, the specific issues of hermeneutical technique. They are the much larger questions of meaning, language, demythologization, and similar matters. The current discussions represent in many ways a continuation of discussions to which Rudolf Bultmann gave a major impetus in 1941 with his essay, "The New Testament and Mythology."

The term "hermeneutics" is used in at least three senses. Perhaps the most common refers to the actual techniques of biblical interpretation. A second sense has to do with the application of these techniques—with the results of that endeavor or the interpretation of the passage. A third sense refers to the whole conception of the nature of the interpretational task. This final sense is generally associated with the strategic issues of hermeneutics; the first sense, with the tactics of hermeneutics. This volume deals with hermeneutics in its third and broadest sense, with the strategy of biblical interpretation, or what one might call philosophical hermeneutics or meta-hermeneutics. It is in no sense a comprehensive textbook of hermeneutics. It is rather a series of essays on important themes of hermeneutics today.

Chapters 1–3 were presented, in somewhat different form, as the Reformation Heritage Lectures at Beeson Divinity School of Samford University, Birmingham, Alabama, October 29–31, 1991. I appreciate greatly the opportunity to deliver the lecture series and the hospitality of the administration and faculty of Beeson, especially its dean, Dr. Timothy George. The response to those lectures was an encouragement to me to prepare the lectures for publication. Chapter 5 was my presidential address at the annual meeting of the Evangelical Philosophical Association, Kansas City, Missouri, November 22, 1991. The responses of my colleagues in that society have helped me sharpen the focus of my thinking.

These essays are sent forth with the prayer that they may contribute to the current discussions of hermeneutics in a way that will help us become more able and accurate interpreters of the incomparable word.

1

The Nature of Authorial Intent

Evangelical hermeneutics of the past quarter-century has placed a great deal of emphasis on the concept of authorial intent. This has been displayed in a number of ways, but one of the clearest and most direct has been the extensive utilization of the thought and writings of E. D. Hirsch, Jr., in evangelical hermeneutics courses.[1] It is also evident in the writings of evangelical teachers of hermeneutics, who insist that a given passage of Scripture has only one meaning, and that this meaning is the meaning intended by the human author. Probably Walter C. Kaiser, Jr., has been the most consistent and insistent in advocating this idea, but others have also sought to make this case persuasively.[2]

The Concern for Single-Meaning Authorial Intent

A number of issues are involved in this concern. One that obviously lay behind Hirsch's writing of *Validity in Interpreta-*

1. Especially his *Validity in Interpretation* (New Haven: Yale University Press, 1967).
2. Kaiser has written so extensively and with so many of the same emphases in his writings that numerous points that he makes could be documented from a large number of sources. In most cases we have given only a single reference to avoid repetitiveness.

tion was the rejection of any type of subjectivism, which would place the locus of meaning in the understanding and interpretation of the reader of the passage. Many types of subjective epistemologies are to be found here, including the two horizons conception of Hans Georg Gadamer. According to this view, the horizon of the biblical author and the horizon of the modern interpreter must merge. Thus, meaning is in a sense the product of the understanding of both the writer and the interpreter.[3] It even extends to postmodern approaches to hermeneutics, such as the "reader-response criticism" advocated by Edgar V. McKnight.[4]

A second view that this emphasis is apparently intended to reject or refute is the Roman Catholic version of the *sensus plenior*, or fuller meaning of Scripture. This conception, in contrast to recent evangelical versions of the doctrine, holds to a considerable extent that the teaching authority of the Catholic Church, the magisterium, makes explicit the meaning or truth that was implicit there from the beginning.

A third stance rejected by this hermeneutical approach is the allegorical interpretation. According to such an understanding, which was popular in the early centuries of Christian theology and finds a prominent place in the thinking of St. Augustine, a given passage of Scripture has no fewer than four meanings: the literal (surface), the moral, the allegorical, and the anagogical.

A fourth approach that seems to be a target of the single-meaning and single-minded thinkers is a form of eschatological hermeneutic that finds dual or multiple meanings within prophetic passages. According to this view, the "real" meaning of the passage may be something quite different from the apparent or surface meaning.

The question we will deal with in this chapter is whether in the desire to reject and refute these views, perceived as erroneous, the authorial intent approach has inadvertently accomplished more than it intended. To do this, we must first

3. Hans Georg Gadamer, *Truth and Method*, 2d rev. ed. (New York: Crossroad, 1990).
4. Edgar V. McKnight, *Postmodern Use of the Bible: The Emergence of Reader-Oriented Criticism* (Nashville: Abingdon, 1988).

examine quite closely the statement of this hermeneutical approach, as well as several responses or alternatives to it. We will then offer an evaluation of the total issue.

The evangelical exegete who has most fully expounded this view is probably Kaiser. The basic tenets of his position can be summarized as follows.

First, the meaning that God has assigned to any passage of Scripture can only be ascertained by studying the verbal meanings of the inspired scriptural writer.[5] This is another way of saying that the divine intention and the intention of the human author are one and the same.

Second, only one verbal meaning is to be assigned to a passage of Scripture unless the author indicates that he has more than one aim in view, an example being the Olivet Discourse.[6]

It is apparent that in this statement Kaiser is linking the Bible with other similar literary works, and essentially treating it as a member of the same class. It is to be interpreted in the same manner and utilizing the same principles as one would for any other book.[7] So he says:

> A literary work like the Bible can have one and only one correct interpretation and that meaning must be determined by the human author's truth-intention; otherwise, all alleged meanings would be accorded the same degree of seriousness, plausibility and correctness with no one meaning being more valid or true than the others.[8]

The strength of expression in Kaiser's writing comes from his sense of the magnitude of the issues involved: the necessity of combating subjectivism in biblical interpretation. He states that even before T. S. Eliot and Ezra Pound,

5. Walter C. Kaiser, Jr., "The Single Intent of Scripture," in *Evangelical Roots: A Tribute to Wilbur Smith*, ed. Kenneth S. Kantzer (Nashville: Thomas Nelson, 1978), p. 138.

6. Ibid.

7. Walter C. Kaiser, Jr., "Legitimate Hermeneutics," in *Inerrancy,* ed. Norman L. Geisler (Grand Rapids: Zondervan, 1980), p. 119.

8. Walter C. Kaiser, Jr., "A Response to Authorial Intention and Biblical Interpretation," in *Hermeneutics, Inerrancy, and the Bible*, ed. Earl D. Radmacher and Robert D. Preus (Grand Rapids: Zondervan, 1984), p. 441.

evangelical exegetical practice had likewise begun to slip into an easygoing subjectivism. Words, events, persons, places, and things in Scripture were allowed to signify all they could be made to signify apart from any authorial controls of those prophets and apostles who claimed to have stood in the divine council and received this intelligible revelation.[9]

Critics of This View

There are, however, those who believe that Kaiser has taken an unnecessary and indefensible position in linking the meaning of the passage to the intention of the human author and by insisting that the author had only one intention, so that the passage can have only one meaning. In their criticisms and in Kaiser's responses we will see more clearly what he intends by his assertion.

One problem with this single authorial intent position, some critics maintain, is that it does not accord with the exegetical practice of the New Testament authors in their treatment of the Old Testament writings. The New Testament interpreters of the Old Testament, in other words, interpreted it as having a different meaning than we would probably find if we did not have the New Testament passage. This is probably most clearly seen with respect to Old Testament prophecy that is fulfilled in the New, although the same dynamic can be seen at work elsewhere as well.

Among some examples are the fulfillment of several statements from Psalms 22 and 69 at the crucifixion of Christ. The cry of "My God, my God, why have you forsaken me?" in Psalm 22:1 was fulfilled in Christ's words from the cross in Matthew 27:46. The words of scorn and shaking of heads in Psalm 22:7 were fulfilled in the treatment of Christ by those who taunted him (Matt. 27:39). The dividing up of garments and casting lots for clothing in Psalm 22:18 were fulfilled at Christ's humiliation (Matt. 27:35); the prediction of gall for food and vinegar for drink (Ps. 69:21) was fulfilled at Christ's suffering on the cross (Matt. 27:34, 48). While each of these psalms has its own historical context and referent, divine inspiration in the writing of the

9. Kaiser, "Single Intent," p. 93.

words of these psalms resulted in their having their fullest meaning in the crucifixion narrative, referring to Jesus.[10] This is also true of a number of typological passages, such as Matthew 2:14–15 (the return of Jesus from Egypt to Israel as a fulfillment of Hos. 11:1), and Matthew 2:16–18 (the slaughter of children in Bethlehem and vicinity as a typological fulfillment of Jer. 31:15).[11]

Here, then, is an interesting phenomenon. If we had only the Old Testament passages, it is unlikely that we would find in them the meaning that the New Testament writers seem to impute to them. If we were Jews rather than Christians, the meaning of the psalmist or the prophet, rather than that of the evangelist, is the one that we would likely understand to be the meaning of the passage. It seems unlikely that the Old Testament writers consciously intended the meaning that Matthew finds in their writings. The explanation of this apparent difference is offered by Jack Riggs: "Matthew saw a fuller sense in those OT passages than was intended by their original authors. This was due to divine revelation given to Matthew by which he saw the correspondence between the OT materials and events in his day."[12]

A second problem with the single-meaning approach, according to its critics, is that there are texts where either the Old Testament writer himself testifies that he does not understand fully what he is writing or a New Testament author says this of an Old Testament author. In 1 Peter 1:10–12, for example, Peter speaks of how the prophets searched intently to try to determine "the time and circumstances to which the Spirit of Christ in them was pointing when he predicted the sufferings of Christ and the glories that would follow." In John 11:49–52, John

10. Donald Hagner, "The Old Testament in the New Testament," in *Interpreting the Word of God*, ed. Samuel J. Schultz and Morris A. Inch (Chicago: Moody, 1976), p. 97.

11. Donald Hagner, "When the Time Had Fully Come," in *Dreams, Visions and Oracles*, ed. Carl W. Armerding and W. Ward Gasque (Grand Rapids: Baker, 1977), pp. 91–93.

12. Jack R. Riggs, "The 'Fuller Meaning' of Scripture: A Hermeneutical Question for Evangelicals," *Grace Theological Journal* 7/2 (Fall 1986): 220. Cf. Hagner, "When the Time Had Fully Come," p. 92.

seems to be saying that Caiaphas, the high priest, prophesied regarding Jesus, without knowing what he was saying.

Third, some critics maintain that the single authorial intent position has difficulty dealing with the relationship between the divine and the human authorship of the Bible. This, of course, has always been an issue for the doctrine of inspiration, but the problem has some unique features in this context. The person who has focused on these problems most extensively is Vern Poythress. He begins with the assumption that the biblical materials are both what God says to us and what the human author says, and then seeks to work out the implications of that stance.[13]

The problem, as Poythress sees it, is especially relevant to the question of how the Bible pertains to our own situation. Rejecting the idea that the divine meaning has nothing to do with the humanly intended meaning, he weighs carefully the idea that the two are simply the same. This solution has some appeal; the problem is that the biblical writers did not write with us directly in view. They did not foresee all of our circumstances and needs. Although we can overhear what they had to say, how are we to know what they want us to do with their words?[14]

A popular solution to the problem, Poythress observes, is the familiar distinction Hirsch draws between meaning and significance. Meaning, on Hirschian grounds, pertains to the assertions of the author; significance has to do with the relation we readers draw between what is said and our own (or others') situation. Application then involves exploring the significance of the teaching for us, and recommending action in accordance with it.[15]

This presents problems, however. Since divine and human authors intended the same meaning, and since the Old Testament writers could not and did not anticipate our situation, it would appear that present-day readers are free to find virtually any significance and make any consequent application they wish. Poythress's initial conclusion is that "when we come to

13. Vern Sheridan Poythress, "Divine Meaning of Scripture," *Westminster Theological Journal* 48/2 (Fall 1986): 241–42.

14. Ibid., p. 244.

15. Ibid., p. 245.

the point of application, we must somewhere along the line appeal directly to God's knowledge, authority, and presence. Otherwise, we are simply 'overhearing' a human voice from long ago, a voice to which we may respond in whatever way suits our own value system."[16]

Poythress traces the problem through a discussion of three different aspects of discourse—the referential, the expressive, and the conative—and grapples with the implications for each of these of the fact that God knows and relates to future readers of the biblical passage in a way that the human author could not. We will come back to some of these considerations later. Here it is sufficient to observe that this is an item for the agenda that Kaiser and others who adopt the Hirschian system must deal with.

A final major problem with the single-meaning approach has to do with the definition of the term "intention." The most extended treatment of this issue has been given by Philip B. Payne. He notes the difficulty in equating divine with human intent in the case of the biblical writings. He maintains that the human authors' meanings may be elusive for several reasons, four of which he specifies:[17]

- the multiplicity of levels at which "intention" can be understood
- the complexity of the writer's intention—the fact that he may have had several reasons for writing what he did
- the fact that intention is a complex category that may involve many different types of states, including the subconscious
- the difficulty of demonstrating the intentions of the biblical authors, since they are removed from us by several centuries of time, and we can only know their thoughts through their writings

16. Ibid., p. 247.
17. Philip B. Payne, "The Fallacy of Equating Meaning with the Human Author's Intention," *Journal of the Evangelical Theological Society* 20/3 (Sept. 1977): 244–46.

The Response to These Criticisms

Having seen these objections to Kaiser's position, we must note how these questions refine Kaiser's statement, or how his statement relates to these concerns. This is not to say that Kaiser explicitly responds to these points in a detailed fashion in every case.

First, Kaiser does not allow for any double meaning of passages. He does hold that there are prophecies that have a single meaning but multiple fulfillments. He believes that this type of prophecy may be understood as generic prophecy, a term and concept that he adopts from Willis J. Beecher. A generic prophecy is one that regards an event as occurring in a series of parts. It may refer to either the nearer or the more remote parts, or to the whole. In referring to the whole, it also refers to the constituent parts.[18]

Second, the passages that seem to teach that the biblical writers were ignorant of the things that they were asserting do not really teach that. For example, in 1 Peter 1:10–12, the author does not profess ignorance of the matters of which he is writing, but only ignorance of the time when these events would occur. The same is true of Daniel 12:6–8. It was not the meaning that was uncertain, but the time of fulfillment. It was the words of the angel, not his own, of which Daniel was speaking. In the case of Caiaphas in John 11:49–52, John found a significance in Caiaphas's words, as distinguished from the meaning that Caiaphas gave to them, and he corrected Caiaphas's provincial meaning.[19]

Third, Kaiser insists that the intention of the human author and that of the divine author correspond. There cannot be any difference between them.[20] He rejects any idea such as that of Bruce Waltke, who advocates interpreting a text in light of the entire Bible, or what Waltke calls "the canonical process approach."[21] If a meaning is found in a passage written later, we

18. Kaiser, "Legitimate Hermeneutics," p. 137.

19. Kaiser, "Single Intent," pp. 125–31.

20. Kaiser, "Response," pp. 445–46.

21. Bruce K. Waltke, "A Canonical Process Approach to the Psalms," in *Tradition and Testament: Essays in Honor of Charles Lee Feinberg*, ed. John and Paul Feinberg (Chicago: Moody, 1981), pp. 3–18.

should go to that passage for the teaching, not try to import it into the earlier passage.[22] Only doctrine and theology written earlier may be legitimately used in the task of theological exegesis, and only where the writer directly cites or obviously alludes to an earlier passage.[23] Kaiser's conclusion is that "God did not exceed the intention of the human author either through a retrojection of the whole of the canon on an earlier text or by means of a hidden freight of meaning which awaited our discovery of it many centuries later."[24]

The remaining issue, that of the levels and complexity of intention of the biblical authors, is one that really does not seem to have been adequately or consciously addressed by Kaiser in any of his numerous writings.

Analysis and Assessment of the Hirschian View

We have now noted the basic statement of the "single-meaning" approach to the doctrine of Scripture and the interpretation thereof. We have also noted some of the objections or statements of an alternative position, as well as Kaiser's responses to these. We must now turn to the examination and evaluation of this hermeneutical stance, and assess its adequacy.

1. First is the problem of framework and terminology. We have noted that Kaiser and other evangelical hermeneuts have adopted Hirsch's terminology and categories. Much of the treatment of the problems raised in relationship to the single-intention view has been handled through the distinction between meaning and significance. This seems to me, however, to be an inaccurate and unduly restrictive treatment of the idea of meaning. Today we often hear people say something like, "That was really meaningful to me." People are searching for meaningful relationships and meaningful experiences. What they are speaking about, however, is what Hirsch and Kaiser would call significance. Kaiser would say they are searching for *significant* relationships, but that is a term that many today would reserve for certain unusual instances of these meaningful relationships.

22. Kaiser, "Response," p. 445.
23. Kaiser, "Single Intent," p. 140.
24. Kaiser, "Response," pp. 445–46.

There are two responses that might well be made to the objection that the Hirsch–Kaiser categories exclude this popular usage. One is that popular usage does not and should not determine correctness or legitimacy. We must bring to bear more informed understandings in assigning terminology. The other response, closely related to the first, is simply that these people are mistaken and that their erroneous notions are to be corrected by a better-informed understanding of Hirsch.

Note, however, that what is being done here is stipulative definition. The choice of terminology excludes any possibility for meaning within the application of the basic tenets. The attempt has been made to win the contest by stating the rules, setting the terms in such a manner that the opposing side has a very difficult time defending its position. It is as if an athletic contest is to be played on a sloping field, with one team being able to stipulate that the contest will be played there and that they will defend the uphill goal for the duration of the game. We must ask whether a different playing field could be chosen, by mutual agreement of both parties. In this case, is there terminology that would be more neutral regarding the outcome, and which also, incidentally, would accord better with ordinary usage, rather than with one theory thereof? In effect we are insisting that conclusions must be argued for, rather than being stipulated, even if indirectly.

It seems to me that a more helpful approach would be to adopt a more inclusive understanding of meaning and then ask which aspect or which variety of meaning applies to the issues under discussion. An analysis of the meaning of meaning would suggest that meaning could be the inclusive term, and that "signification" would be used of what Hirsch and Kaiser call meaning, with "significance" retaining approximately the same definition that they give it.[25]

2. A second concern associated with the single-meaning stance centers on the understanding of intention. Part of the problem is the need for a more precise definition of intention. It

25. I find, for example, the theory of semiotic proposed by Charles Morris to be considerably more inclusive while at the same time less confusing and ambiguous. See his *Signification and Significance: A Study of the Relations of Signs and Values* (Cambridge, Mass.: MIT, 1964).

does appear, however, from Kaiser's use of the term, that he has in mind conscious intention, or what the person consciously wills to do (in this case, what the writer consciously wills to communicate). The constant objection to anyone "writing better than he knew" seems to stem from such an understanding.

We must now ask ourselves, however, whether we ever communicate anything that we do not consciously intend to communicate. The proverbial Freudian slip suggests that this is indeed the case, as is true also of body language and other forms of nonverbal communication. Those who are skilled in the interpretation of such aspects of behavior can often discern communication that we do not consciously intend and perhaps would not even want to communicate. We may not even understand why we did what we did. A former colleague of mine in the field of pastoral care used to say quite frequently, "You cannot *not* communicate."

We must also ask whether we ever say, think, or do something that we were not aware of prior to the moment of so doing. I remember my family's first day in Sweden. We had stopped to arrange for a room in a pensionnat, and my second daughter, who had studied Swedish, went in with me to help in the negotiations. To her surprise (and mine), however, I was quite capable of handling the arrangements unaided, including asking for directions to the local church. When we got out to the car, she said, "Dad, you spoke more Swedish than you know!" Words that had been buried in my unconscious since my grandmother died thirty-six years before, had come back into consciousness.

The illustration, of course, seems to break down. Kaiser would say that I did not speak better than I knew; I just did not know that I knew. The point, however, is that there is a considerable reservoir of unconscious material in the personalities of all of us. "Depth psychology" maintains that sometimes we communicate without knowing what we are communicating, and even without knowing the fact (usually about ourselves) that we are communicating.

The Hirsch–Kaiser understanding of intention appears to be a pre-twentieth-century understanding of psychology. It proceeds as if Freud had never written. Now it may, of course, be

21

argued that this is a virtue, that this keeps us from a corrupting understanding of human psychology. This seems to me an attempt to preserve or conserve something that our theology or the teaching of Scripture does not require us to maintain. As such, it is the maintenance of a particular theory that has been attached to our theology, rather than an essential part of it. The objection to this aspect of the psychoanalytic view is less like the church's objection to Darwinism as a complete explanation of the origin of life in all its forms, including the human, and more like its resistance to the Copernican revolution.

A skilled counselor does not tell the client the truth, but helps the client discover that truth. In this sense, the counselor is helping the client understand what he or she is saying without realizing that he or she is saying it. All of us have probably had the experience of someone else understanding what we have said better than we ourselves. Typically, the other person says, "In other words, you mean . . . ?" and our response is, "Yes, I guess that *is* what I meant." These are experiences of genuine insight into what we actually meant, not merely of expressing more adequately what we were consciously intending to say.

Hirsch's concept of unconscious meaning appears to challenge this. He states that "the fact that verbal meaning has to have some kind of boundary in order to be communicable and capable of valid interpretation does not exclude so-called unconscious meaning."[26] He goes on to say that "the principle for excluding or accepting unconscious meaning is precisely the same as for conscious ones."[27] Since, however, the criterion of meaning is that which the author intends, we appear to be saying here that the author's intention may include that of which he or she is not aware. It is simply necessary that the person wills this, whether he or she attends to it or not. We cannot will something against our will, for that would be a contradiction. It is only necessary that there be some connection between the unconscious and the conscious aspects of the will to make intention voluntary.[28]

26. Hirsch, *Validity*, p. 51.
27. Ibid.
28. Ibid., pp. 51–52.

Note, however, what has become of the concept of intention. It applies to that which one chooses without being aware of what he or she is choosing. It seems to exclude only such "symptoms" as stuttering. But there seems to be a dual problem here. On the one hand, the concept of intention has been stretched to include unconscious intention, involving such elasticity of meaning (yes, meaning, on Hirsch's terms) as to make the term virtually meaningless. On the other hand, the exclusion of such unwilled utterances as stuttering seems to save the term "intention" from utter meaninglessness. Yet from some perspectives, this seems to be a rather arbitrary exclusion. For if the psychoanalysts are right, then much of the other unconscious meaning communicated is just as involuntary as stuttering. If not, then we are back to the seeming contradiction of intention without consciousness. In any event, the Hirschian conceptuality seems to be in need of some adjustment.

I would propose that a better terminology would be to speak of that which the author "affirms." This would focus on the product of the intending, rather than the process, and would avoid any appearance of conscious intention as a requisite for meaning.

3. Another problem with the single-meaning approach to Scripture is the relevance of a biblical passage for those coming after the group to which the original saying or writing was given. Since the author presumably did not have them within his intent, what meaning for them can there be in his writing?

Basically, the means of handling this problem is through the meaning/significance distinction. The author's intended meaning is the meaning, while the application of that meaning to later audiences is a question of significance. This solution preserves the unity of meaning, while allowing for a diversity of readers to benefit from the teaching. It is a case of one meaning, with many applications.

The challenge, of course, is to get from the past meaning to the present significance. Kaiser is to be commended for making a concerted and thorough effort to do this, and he has done it in an effective way. His basic method, after having thoroughly determined the author's meaning through a careful examination of the exegetical considerations, is to "principlize" the teaching, or to seek to determine the underlying principles within the teaching. These principles can then be reapplied to the present situation, thus yielding significance.

The problem then becomes, however, what it is that the biblical writer intended. Did he intend the specific form of the expression, or the underlying timeless truth? To use one of Kaiser's examples, what was the intent of the biblical author in Numbers 22?

> Balaam sought
> Balaam fought
> Balaam taught?

Or is it that we can know and do the will of God

> by keeping the faith
> by obeying God's Word
> by observing the obstacles?[29]

Is the latter "meant" or "intended" by the author, or only the former? If it is meant, is it meant in addition to the former (which would seem to give a dual meaning to the text), or is it, rather than the former, what is the real intention of the author?

One way of dealing with the problem is to say that the former is the meaning and the latter is the significance. The analysis is not as simple as that, however. In many cases, the original writing of the author also includes the significance for the original hearers or readers. Then the question becomes even more acute. Was the original intent of the author to give both meaning and significance? And what is the relationship of the author to the timeless truth or principles?

Part of the difficulty here comes from lack of clarity regarding the relationship between principles and significance. Principles are timeless truths, significant not for any particular readers but for all persons at all times. The sermon outlines that Kaiser offers are not contextualized to our time or situation or to any particular time or situation. There really is nothing in

29. Walter C. Kaiser, Jr., *Toward an Exegetical Theology: Biblical Exegesis for Preaching and Teaching* (Grand Rapids: Baker, 1981), p. 158.

these outlines that could not have been preached in just that way two hundred or one thousand years ago. The outlines that he offers differ from the outlines of the text, but not to a radical degree. They are not really sufficiently removed from the exegetical outlines to qualify as homiletical outlines. This is seen, for example, in the proposal that the order of the subpoints should follow the order of the text.[30] Kaiser's outlines do not include specific applications.

It might be better to think of the types of activity that Kaiser describes in his *Toward an Exegetical Theology* as exegesis and pure exposition, respectively, and then recognize another classification of such activity, namely, expository preaching. This third activity would include specific application to the concrete situation of persons today. Despite his desire to get the message all the way to the present day, it seems that Kaiser has only succeeded in getting to the timeless status, leaving the application to the contemporary Christian and the Holy Spirit to work out between them. He has only gotten specific at those points where the Bible is specific; it would seem that there has been no change in the situation important enough to alter the application. This neglect, however, seems to stem from Kaiser's adoption of Hirschian categories, so that he denies the idea of meaning to anything beyond the immediate statement of the author.

For Hirsch, the problem is dealt with through the concept of implication: what the author intends includes the implications thereof.[31] Here again, however, we must ask about just what Hirsch is affirming. Does the author intend the literal, specific statement, or the underlying principles? To take a biblical example, what was the author of Genesis 22:1–19 intending to tell us? On the surface of it, it seems that he was intending to tell us that God commanded Abraham to sacrifice his son, Isaac, that Abraham obeyed, and that God then provided a sacrificial animal as a substitute, thus enabling the promised heir, Isaac, to be preserved.

But what of the timeless truth? Did the author also intend to tell us that God expects obedience, and that he is faithful to his promises? That is not necessarily part of what he consciously

30. Ibid., p. 160.
31. Hirsch, *Validity*, pp. 61–67.

25

intended, but it seems to be an implication. We must, however, ask which of these two meanings the author intends. Either we have a dual meaning, or meaning has again become quite elastic. The concept of implication appears to expand considerably the concept of intention. I believe it would be preferable to say that the author affirmed the former, but that it implies the latter. The original incident with Abraham is an instance of this principle. It also, however, can be instantiated or contextualized in other situations in our own and other times.

4. Another problem is the tendency to equate meaning with then and significance with now. This analysis is inadequate, however. We have already pointed out that the original text had significance for the original audience. There should therefore be original significance and consequent significance. Beyond that, however, we need to grapple with the issue of signification then and signification now. Some of what was said at that time would "mean" something different now. What would eating meat offered to idols or a woman shaving her head mean now? Kaiser would probably say that these are significances for people today of meaning from the past, but was there not also significance for that time? Here again the ambiguity regarding what is intended by the author manifests itself.

5. Yet another problem appears to be a limitation of the type of meaning to just one type, namely, the referential. Poythress has discussed several types of meaning, including the expressive and the conative. There seems here to be a strong emphasis on the cognitive rather than the affective dimensions of communication and experience. The affective and volitional dimensions of experience come in only as application or significance, which is not "meaning."

This limitation of meaning shows itself in a number of ways. One is in the depreciation of the sermon introduction, as contrasted with the conclusion: "We need to reevaluate our priorities in this matter of introductions. I would urge God's ministers and teachers of the Word in every type of ministry inside and outside of the Church to severely limit their work on the introduction and to devote that time and those energies of preparation to an expanded and clearly-thought-out conclusion."[32]

32. Kaiser, *Toward an Exegetical Theology*, p. 163.

There is a real point to this suggestion, to a certain degree. A sermon that simply presents the truth and then leaves hearers to make their own application is incomplete. A sermon's application should not be restricted to the conclusion, however, but should be present throughout the message. Beyond that, lack of information is only one part of the problem. Another problem, and often the larger one in our age, is lack of interest. It is this that the introduction is intended to deal with: the introduction is meant to attract the attention of the hearers, to overcome antipathy, to help those listening see that the sermon will be of value to them.[33] In short, the communication must deal with affective as well as cognitive dimensions.

Even the pastor's role in communicating God's Word has been truncated. The proverbial neglect of the exegetical use of the biblical languages is traced to the failure to teach seminarians how to identify what in the word "remains normative and authoritative to the present moment."[34] Kaiser alludes to the problem of the demands on a pastor's time, but there still seems to be the assumption that the communication of biblical truth is primarily accomplished through the formal sermon. While it is important that the layperson receive a message that is a faithful rendition of the true meaning of the biblical text, there are other needs besides the cognitive. The single-meaning approach does not seem to do adequate justice to those other dimensions of meaning. As important as sermons are, the communication of the biblical reality of Christianity often is accomplished more effectively in counseling and in hospital visitation than in the pulpit ministry. And again, the problem with lack of communication may be just as much a failure to *hear* the biblical truth as a failure to hear the *biblical truth*. The conative and affective ministries outside the pulpit may be what make sermons effective. As one pastor put it, "They won't care what you know, until they know that you care."

I find it very easy as a pastor and theologian to project my own perspective on laypeople. Thus, I evaluate a sermon in terms of whether a seminary professor will appreciate it. I have

---

33. Michael J. Hostetler, *Introducing the Sermon: The Art of Compelling Beginnings* (Grand Rapids: Zondervan, 1986).

34. Ibid., p. 132.

to remind myself when I go to church that if I am completely pleased with the sermon, it probably was not a good sermon for the congregation, most of whom are not seminary professors. (Indeed, full-time faculty members at accredited theological schools in the United States constitute only .012 percent of the population.) There are a few very gifted preachers who can communicate effectively on several different levels at the same time.

6. The single-meaning approach does not deal adequately with the complexity of communication. It leads to the erroneous assumption that there is only one central meaning of the passage, and that this meaning is the only possible subject of the lesson or the sermon. That one central truth, however, is frequently the conclusion of an argument. What about the supporting assertions? Did the author intend to present those as well, and if so, can they not be sermon topics as well?

For example, we have Jesus' teaching about providence in Matthew 10, in which he points out God's protection of birds (v. 29) and then goes on to observe that his human hearers are of more value than many sparrows. The conclusion is that God will take care of his human children. What did the author (Matthew) intend to communicate, and for that matter, what did Jesus intend? Was it only the value of humans and God's care for them, or was it also the value of birds and other members of the creation and God's care for them? Is the "big idea" the only idea in the passage that can be the subject of a sermon?[35] Can we also use this passage as a basis for a message on animal rights, or ecology, or divine providence as it applies to human beings? This issue has not been adequately thought through, and the conclusions being followed hardly seem adequately justified by argument.

7. The hermeneutic developed here also seems to break down when it is confronted by certain types of biblical material, most conspicuously, prophecy. That a New Testament writer should present a meaning other than the prophet intended is a challenge. The solution that Kaiser has adopted is Willis J. Beecher's "generic prediction/promise." This approach "regards an event

35. Haddon Robinson, *Biblical Preaching: The Development and Delivery of Expository Messages* (Grand Rapids: Baker, 1980), pp. 31–48.

as occurring in a series of parts, separated by intervals, and expresses itself in language that may apply indifferently to the nearest part, or to the more remote parts, or to the whole—in other words, a prediction which, in applying to the whole of a complex event, also applies to some of its parts."[36]

This attempt to account for a New Testament writer's application of an Old Testament prophecy, without accepting the idea of a double sense or multiple meanings, is a rather feeble attempt to avoid the problem. It fails to point out that the author regarded the prediction in this way, and to demonstrate that in each of the instances.

Discussions about the hermeneutical problem seem to center primarily on Old Testament prophecies and their fulfillment in the New Testament. The New Testament authors tend to give interpretations of these prophecies, which, like their treatment of other Old Testament quotations, seem to be somewhat at variance with the interpretation that we would otherwise have given to the passages.

There is still a further problem, however, with prophecies, whether from the Old or the New Testament, which have not yet been fulfilled. When we look at these prophecies and attempt to interpret them, it is sometimes difficult to assert that the intention of the human author was identical with the divine intention, or, to put it differently, that the human author was fully conscious of the meaning of what he was writing.

Take, for instance, John's prophecy involving the seven seals (Rev. 6–8). Just what was his intention in writing this? Was he simply telling his readers about seven seals? Did he know what all of these things meant? It may well be that he was given the meaning of these seals, but there is nothing in the passage to indicate that. Is there meaning beyond the vision and John's apparent intention to tell what he had viewed and experienced (the expressive meaning of the passage)? Was there something more, of a referential nature? If so, where is its locus within the passage? How does that meaning relate to the symbols that John used?

36. Walter C. Kaiser, Jr., "The Promise of Isaiah 7:14 and the Single-Meaning Hermeneutic," *Evangelical Journal* 6/3 (Fall 1988): 66.

Just as we might say that God was implying other meanings beyond the literal meanings of the symbols, so we could also say that John was given an insight into the meaning but did not convey it to his hearers. The problem here, however, is that God presumably has a knowledge of the future that far exceeds that of the author or any other human. This knowledge, however, is not merely information that humans do not have, but also involves even the categories that a human who had not experienced the future would not ordinarily have. Thus, for the human author to intend what God intends, it would be necessary for him to be given an extensive knowledge of the future to provide a framework within which to understand it and thus to consciously intend what he was going to write. There is really no indication of the writer possessing this extensive sort of revelation, which would presumably have produced some sense of being overwhelmed.

8. It appears that at the root of the several problems described above as well as a number of others that we have not treated here is the adoption of a methodology without due attention to the compatibility of its presuppositions with those of the Christian biblical tradition. The aim of Hirsch, and of Kaiser and other like-minded evangelical hermeneuts, is to reject or avoid the type of subjectivism in which the meaning of the text is whatever meaning the reader finds in it, or whatever "speaks to" the reader from the text. The other aim seems to be to avoid any form of the Roman Catholic approach, which holds that God has given continuing and fuller revelation through the church, and that its magisterium therefore can reveal the meaning of the text.

In so doing, however, more has been accomplished than was intended. Hirsch articulates no doctrine of the Holy Spirit, for he is dealing with generic literature, not necessarily the Bible. The author of the writings he is dealing with is solely the human author. When Kaiser says that the rules governing the interpretation of the Bible are simply those governing any writing, he is essentially accepting the assumption that the Bible was written like any other book. Although he struggles mightily to correlate human authorship with divine inspiration, a built-in contradiction continues to surface. The antisupernaturalist (or at least nonsupernaturalist) assumptions eliminate any meaning conveyed by a divine coauthor of which the human author would not be consciously aware. This also excludes effectively any role for the Holy Spirit in the interpretational process, a problem that we will examine more closely in a subsequent treatment.

Needed Modifications and Correctives

Having engaged in this protracted critique of the authorial intent position, what can we offer by way of a corrective?

For the most part, I am in agreement with Kaiser and Hirsch. The subjective or reader-response type of interpretation that they oppose is an insidious movement, which ultimately results in the breakdown of all meaning, or at least, of shared meaning. That the text has a meaning independent of anyone hearing, reading, or interpreting it, must be insisted upon. Certain modifications are needed, however.

First, the term "intention" is too ambiguous, and could well be replaced by "affirmation." Intention can be too easily confused with consciousness or with psychologistic concepts. Hirsch recognizes this, and qualifies the statement repeatedly, to include meanings of which the author is not aware, and "types," which include all members possessing the traits common to the type, subsuming implication within meaning. The terminology becomes so elastic that it dies Antony Flew's famous "death of a thousand qualifications."[37] The term "assertion" refers to what the author actually wrote, rather than what he intended to write. It still emphasizes the act of the writer in producing the writing, but focuses on the product rather than the process.

Second, the concept of authorship needs to be expanded to consciously allow for the role of the Holy Spirit, the inspirer, as a coauthor of Scripture.

Third, the terms "meaning" and "significance" could profitably be replaced by "signification" and "significance," respec-

---

37. Antony Flew, "Theology and Falsification," in *New Essays in Philosophical Theology*, ed. Antony Flew and Alisdair MacIntyre (New York: Macmillan, 1955), p. 97.

tively. This would remove the tendency to identify the former with meaning then and the latter with meaning now. It would also allow the affirmed meaning to include future persons and situations, as well as those to whom the writing was immediately addressed.

Finally, the principle of Scripture interpreting Scripture needs to be relied on, not simply by pointing to biblical passages in which antecedent Scripture is overtly utilized. In conjunction with this, the concept of the authorship of Scripture by the Holy Spirit must be sufficiently emphasized.

2

The Role of the Holy Spirit in Biblical Interpretation

One doctrine that until recently has received relatively little attention is the doctrine of illumination. As traditionally understood, this doctrine teaches that the Holy Spirit of God does a supernatural work of grace in the believer's mind and life, making possible understanding of the Scripture that He has inspired. Illumination is necessary because of sin's effect on the noetic powers of human beings. Some of the countering of this blindness takes place at the point of new birth, but some of it is a direct spiritual work at the point of exposure to the content of Scripture.

The Hermeneutical Stance of Daniel Fuller

More recently, a radically different view of the role of the Holy Spirit has arisen. According to this view, the Holy Spirit's real role is not giving cognition, or knowledge of the meaning of Scripture, but making possible the reception of that truth. Perhaps the clearest and most definite statement of this position has been given by Daniel P. Fuller.

Fuller begins by noting that some in the history of the church have relied on the Holy Spirit in contrast to methods of determining the verbal meaning of the text. Origen, for example, insisted that since the writers of the Bible were inspired by the Holy Spirit to give them the content of the Scripture that they wrote, the interpreter must also be taught by the Holy Spirit. This will enable the interpreter to go beyond the historical-grammatical data or the literal meaning of the Bible to its spiritual meaning. This spiritual meaning is an allegorical or typological meaning. Fuller observes that "The problem with this understanding of the role of the Holy Spirit in biblical interpretation is that the words of the text can play no essential role in conveying its intended meaning, even though it is these very words which the writers were inspired to use in transmitting God's message to men."[1]

This idea fits the understanding of 1 Corinthians 2:13–14: the divine message was uttered by the biblical spokesmen "not in words taught us by human wisdom, but in words taught by the Spirit" and can be received and known only by those indwelt by the Holy Spirit. Fuller, however, asks what this role of the Holy Spirit is. He also wonders: "How does this role urge the exegete always to acknowledge his complete dependence on the Holy Spirit, and at the same time urge him to develop his skill in using valid exegetical means to determine the meanings that were intended by the words which the Holy Spirit inspired the biblical writer to use?"[2]

Fuller believes that the answer to the question will be found in a closer examination of 1 Corinthians 2:14. His interpretation can be summarized as follows.

1. The problem involved in the rejection of the spiritual message is not lack of understanding, but lack of willingness. The difficulty, in other words, is not intellectual but volitional. The correct understanding of "receive" can be seen in the meaning of the Greek verb *dechomai,* which is used here rather than *lambanō*. Whereas *lambanō* means simply to receive something, *dechomai* means "to accept some requested offering willingly and with pleasure." So when Paul says that the natural man does not receive the things of the Spirit of God, the real meaning

---

1. Daniel P. Fuller, "The Holy Spirit's Role in Biblical Interpretation," in *Scripture, Tradition, and Interpretation*, ed. W. Ward Gasque and William Sanford LaSor (Grand Rapids: Eerdmans, 1978), p. 190.
2. Ibid.

is that "apart from the Holy Spirit, a person does not accept what the Bible teaches with pleasure, willingness, and eagerness. In other words, the natural man does not welcome the things of the Spirit of God."[3] This does not exclude, but actually requires, a cognition of what the natural man repudiates. A person cannot feel revulsion when encountering a biblical teaching without first understanding it. A person cannot hate something without having some knowledge of it.[4]

The statement that "spiritual things are foolishness to the natural man" does not mean that the biblical teachings are unintelligible, like an unknown language would be. Rather, these "spiritual things" are understood but regarded as false. An example would be Paul's encounter with Festus (Acts 26:4–23). Festus regarded Paul as "insane." He certainly had to understand what Paul said, however, in order to be able to reject it.[5]

It seems as if Paul's statement that the natural man cannot know the things of the Spirit of God, because they are spiritually discerned would present problems for Fuller's theology. Fuller acknowledges that *ginōskō* can represent the idea of merely perceiving. In general, however, it means "embracing things as they really are." If used in this sense in the second half of the verse, the meaning would be a close parallel to the earlier statement that the natural man does not welcome spiritual things.[6]

What about the explanation that the natural man does not "accept" spiritual things "because they are spiritually discerned"? Fuller says that the Greek word here for "discerned" is *anakinō* [sic] and that it represents "an investigative action carried on for the purpose of rendering an appraisal or evaluation."[7] He believes that this supports the idea that the problem is inability to see the worth or value, rather than the meaning, of biblical teachings. He says, "One's inability to welcome spiritual things is supported more aptly by affirming that he cannot evaluate them than by affirming that he cannot even have cognition of them."[8]

3. Ibid., p. 191.
4. Ibid.
5. Ibid.
6. Ibid.
7. Ibid., pp. 191–92.
8. Ibid., p. 192.

2. A major conclusion follows from this. The Holy Spirit's role in biblical interpretation does not consist in giving the interpreter cognition of what the Bible is saying, which would involve dispensing additional information beyond the historical-grammatical data that are already there for everyone to work with: "Rather, the Holy Spirit's role is to change the heart of the interpreter, so that he loves the message that is conveyed by nothing more than the historical-grammatical data."[9] This means that the biblical interpreter does not expect the Holy Spirit to give him the meaning of the text. He must work diligently to develop his exegetical skills and use them effectively in the hard work of understanding a text.[10]

3. The problem that an unbeliever has with the text does not affect his ability to understand it correctly. While a biblical text may conflict with his value systems, that conflict does not affect the accuracy of his exegesis. The agnostic or atheist seeks simply to describe academically what the Bible says; he does not do this in order to influence his own values and actions. Fuller notes, in fact, that "an agnostic or an atheist, whose concern is simply to set forth, say, a description of Pauline thought, can make a lasting contribution to this subject, if he has achieved a high degree of exegetical skill."[11] He quotes with favor Krister Stendahl, who states that agnostics and believers can work side by side, "since no other tools are called for than those of description in the terms indicated by the texts themselves."[12]

4. The values taught in Scripture, however, conflict with those of the natural human being. This conflict affects adversely the ability of the unsanctified believer to interpret the biblical text correctly. When we move from descriptive biblical theology as an end in itself to the study of the text to give meaning and purpose to life, things change. In this situation there is a tendency to modify the meanings of the Bible to make them palatable. "Such hermeneutical gambits as demythologizing, or interpreting a passage of the Bible from some religious a priori, or

9. Ibid.
10. Ibid.
11. Ibid.
12. Ibid.

interpreting one biblical passage in the terms of another—these are some of the ways people commonly justify modifying the meaning of a text that would stand simply by letting its pertinent historical-grammatical data speak for themselves."[13]

5. Although he does not explicitly draw this conclusion, the implication of what Fuller has said is that, other things being equal, a capable unbelieving exegete will be better able to understand cognitively the biblical message than will a relatively unsanctified believing exegete. The apparent foolishness of the Scripture stems from the fact that the gospel allows no room for boasting. As long as we are striving to overcome our own finiteness so that we can delight in trusting in ourselves, our natural reaction will be to denounce the Bible's teaching. It is in terms of the reaction to this conflict that the contrast between the unbelieving and the believing exegete is made apparent. On the one hand,

> these doctrines will present no problem to those whose only concern in biblical interpretation is to give an accurate description of biblical theology. . . . So they have no need to modify the teachings determined by the pertinent historical-grammatical data of the Bible, and to the extent that they are skilled in exegesis, their exposition of what the biblical writers intended to say will be accurate.[14]

On the other hand, "those who expound the teachings of the Bible as true will refrain from modifying the intended meanings of the biblical writers only as their desire for ego-satisfaction is replaced by a delight in God's faithfulness to keep his promises."[15]

Analysis of Fuller's Position

We must now look at several presuppositions that underlie Fuller's thinking and affect the conclusions that he draws. This analysis should assist us in understanding what he is saying and why he is saying it, as well as prepare us for an evaluation

13. Ibid., p. 193.
14. Ibid., p. 197.
15. Ibid.

of his position. Fuller's assumptions lie in several different areas and are of several different types.

1. Fuller assumes that there is a disjunctive relationship between the use of methods of scientific exegesis to get at the historical-grammatical data, and reliance on the Holy Spirit to give insight. This assumption is revealed in his opening statement in which he refers to those in the history of the church who "have insisted that the proper understanding of a passage in the Bible is gained only by those who go beyond the wording of the text and seek the illumination that the Holy Spirit provides."[16] His selection of Origen to represent the position to which he is opposed underscores this assumption. The problem with this approach, Fuller believes, is that "the words of the text can play no essential role in conveying its intended meaning."[17]

2. Fuller also assumes that sin affects our volitional rather than noetic powers. The unbelieving exegete, then, is not hindered at all in a cognitive ability to know the meaning of the passage.

Assessments of moral action generally require that at least three components be satisfied in order to fulfill the right. First, we must correctly know what is right. Rationalists like Plato believed that if the right was correctly known, it would inevitably be done. Second, we must will to do what is right. Third, we must have the ability to do the right, once we have known and chosen it. In Fuller's analysis, sin seems to have its locus in the second of these areas, the ability to choose and to will.

3. Another of Fuller's assumptions is that the different aspects of human personality, or different faculties, to use the traditional terminology, may interact with each other, but they need not. The person is not a unitary being. Interestingly, he seems to favor the idea that the volitional affects the cognitive more than vice versa. The conflict of the biblical teaching with the natural desire for self-glorification affects the ability of the believer to understand the truth of the biblical teaching, but exposure to the truth does not affect the adoption of the values by the unbeliever.

16. Ibid., p. 189.
17. Ibid., p. 190.

In one sense Fuller's view is very rationalistic, and in another, or perhaps two other senses, it is not. It is rationalistic, theologically, in the sense that human reason or rationality is very much intact. On the other hand, Fuller is apparently skeptical about the power of the intellect to recognize the truth when confronted with it. And the power of the intellect to affect the will seems to be less than the power of the will to affect the intellect (at least its ability to recognize the truth). Another way of putting this is that in Fuller's view the effect of original sin on the mind is not direct, but indirect. The corruption of the will causes it to distort the intellect's appreciation of the truth.

4. Fuller also assumes that there is basically one level of understanding of biblical meaning. The level of knowledge is that of the grammatical-exegetical meaning of the text. There is no element here of discernment as a deeper insight into the text, or of heart knowledge as contrasted with head knowledge, or anything of that type. At this level of knowledge the ability of the human to acquire knowledge is not affected by the effects of sin on the human personality.

5. Fuller also seems to assume that exegesis is presuppositionless. The fact that the unbeliever may come with a very different worldview than does the believer apparently does not affect in any significant way the former's understanding of the biblical text. There is no hint here of differing cultural backgrounds contributing differing presuppositions that might govern what is discovered in the text.

6. Finally, for Fuller the understanding of the nature of biblical theology is that of the descriptive approach. This is seen in his repudiation of any approach in which one biblical passage is interpreted in terms of another.

It is quite possible to do biblical theology on this level. The application of these matters to life is something that the believer is likely to do, but biblical theology simply as a recounting of what was believed in biblical times is a legitimate activity. This relating of the biblical teachings to other issues would seem to be something more than biblical theology.

Evaluation of Fuller's Position

We need now to proceed to evaluate this view. There are a number of areas in which Fuller's theory appears to be inadequate.

1. First, there are exegetical problems with Fuller's approach. He claims that his position is supported by the exegesis of 1 Corinthians 2, especially verse 14. We need to submit that contention to close scrutiny, however.

The Greek word *dechomai* does indeed carry the idea of receiving or accepting, as contrasted with *lambanō*, which has a somewhat more passive sense of simply receiving. It does connote the idea of approval. What the word in itself cannot tell us, however, is the basis of that approval or disapproval. It may be that those who would receive understand but reject what is there because they find it disagreeable; or it may be that failing to understand they do not know whether they wish to receive it or not. In other words, the basis of disapproval may be conscious rejection or refusal, or it may be simple failure to accept.

The Greek word *ginōskō* is even more problematic for Fuller's view. It appears to mean the cognitive knowledge of things, facts, or persons. It lacks something of the personal dimension of *oida*. There is little of the valuational dimension that Fuller requires.[18]

Fuller maintains that the word *anakrinō* conveys the idea of an investigative action aimed at rendering an appraisal or evaluation, seeing the worth of something. The word as used elsewhere in Scripture, however, seems to involve an intensive search to determine the meaning of the Scriptures. It is used, for example, of the Bereans, who searched the Scriptures eagerly (Acts 17:11). It is intensity of investigation that seems to be involved in the meaning. It is used of judicial investigations, a biblical instance of which is found in 1 Corinthians 4:3. It involves discernment. The idea that emerges most compellingly from these instances is of investigation aimed at coming to understand that which goes beyond mere surface meaning.

18. See Walter Bauer, *A Greek-English Lexicon of the New Testament*, translated, adapted, and augmented by William F. Arndt and F. Wilbur Gingrich (Chicago: University of Chicago Press, 1979), pp. 160–62.

Is there not an indication, however, in 1 Corinthians 3:19, that this impression of foolishness is not a matter of cognitive understanding? Paul says that the wisdom of humans is foolishness to God. Certainly, however, an omniscient God cannot fail to understand the things of humans. Exegetical sensitivity should lead us to recognize satire in this statement; it is as if God says, "What you call wisdom, I actually see to be foolishness." God, being omniscient, sees the inadequacy of our limited reasoning.

2. There also are biblical difficulties with this approach in a broader sense of biblical. The teaching that Fuller claims to find in the passage contradicts other teachings on the same subject. Here, of course, his view of biblical theology as descriptive would ordinarily lead us to say, "This is Paul's view, as contrasted with that of John," or "This is Paul's understanding at this point, as contrasted with another point in his development." Fuller, however, seems to want to go beyond the purely descriptive to a more normative approach. That ordinarily involves saying, "And this is to be my view," which in turn requires a somewhat more universal type of conception, a view of the truth status of the contention as applying irrespective of the viewpoint of the individual.

In the extended discourse on the Holy Spirit Jesus gives to his disciples (John 14–16), he makes several assertions about the work of the Spirit that seem to involve granting understanding that those who do not have the Spirit will not receive: he "will teach you all things and will remind you of everything I have said to you" (14:26); "testify about me" (15:26); "guide you into all truth" (16:13); "take from what is mine and make it known to you" (16:15). These assertions seem to indicate a work of the Holy Spirit relative to the cognitive dimension of the human.

Does this not abstract more from the passage than should be done, however? Was Jesus not simply promising these blessings to the immediate circle of disciples, telling them what the Spirit would do within their lifetimes? The completion of the revelation and thus of the New Testament canon would occur to and through them and their contemporaries, and this was the means by which that completion would occur.

These statements have to be seen in their context, however. If Jesus meant them to be only for his immediate disciples, what about the other teachings and promises in the passage? Unless there is some sufficient basis for distinguishing these from the ones we have already examined, they too must be restricted to the immediate hearers of the promises. Was the Comforter to be with them forever, but only with them (14:16–17)? Was he to be with and dwell in only them (14:17)? Would he only convict or convince of sin, righteousness, and judgment those to whom they presented the message (16:7–11)? What about the other promises Jesus gave here, independent of his reference to the Holy Spirit? Among these are, "I will do whatever you ask in my name, so that the Son may bring glory to the Father. You may ask me for anything in my name, and I will do it" (14:13–14); "He who loves me will be loved by my Father, and I too will love him and show myself to him" (14:21); "I am going there to prepare a place for you. And if I go and prepare a place for you, I will come back and take you to be with me that you also may be where I am" (14:2–3); "My Father will love him, and we will come to him and make our home with him" (14:23); "Peace I leave with you; my peace I give you. I do not give to you as the world gives. Do not let your hearts be troubled and do not be afraid" (14:27); "You are already clean because of the word I have spoken to you. Remain in me, and I will remain in you" (15:3–4); "If a man remains in me and I in him, he will bear much fruit; apart from me you can do nothing" (15:5); "If you remain in me and my words remain in you, ask whatever you wish, and it will be given you" (15:7). Other promises appear in 15:10, 15, 16; 16:22, 23, 24, 27, 33.

There are, to be sure, some elements of the discourse that appear to be specifically directed to that group of disciples: "they will put you out of the synagogue" (16:2); "In a little while you will see me no more, and then after a little while you will see me" (16:16). These, however, seem to be fairly clearly related to their circumstances. The other promises, however, are so intertwined with apparently universal or perpetual promises, that it would be difficult to restrict them to the immediate situation, unless there were some specific contextual reason for making such a distinction. From these considerations it appears that the teaching about the illumination of the Holy Spirit was not simply restricted to that generation.

Another significant passage is 2 Corinthians 4:3–4, which powerfully portrays the difference between the situation of the believer and that of the unbeliever. Speaking of the presentation of the gospel, Paul says, "And even if our gospel is veiled, it is veiled to those who are perishing. The god of this age has blinded the minds of unbelievers, so that they cannot see the light of the gospel of the glory of Christ." This is a very different picture than that drawn by Fuller. There is an inability to see, even though the light is there. There is a veiling, a blinding. This is more than just understanding but rejecting something because it does not comport with one's self-interest. This is an inability even to understand the truth.

Contrasted with this is the description of the believer: "For God, who said, 'Let light shine out of darkness,' made his light shine in our hearts to give us the light of the knowledge of the glory of God in the face of Christ" (v. 6). It is the believer who is able clearly to see the truth, not the unbeliever.

This inability to understand must also be seen in the context of the preceding passage. There Paul is especially referring to the Israelites. He describes them as having a veil placed over their hearts. His statement, then, is significant: "But whenever anyone turns to the Lord, the veil is taken away" (3:16). He goes on to speak of how those with unveiled faces will all reflect the Lord's glory (v. 18).

These statements constitute a strong indication that there is both a veiling or blinding and an unveiling or illumination. Bernard Ramm's comment on these verses draws exactly the opposite conclusion from that drawn by Fuller:

> When our minds are blinded by the god of this world, everything we read in the New Testament may be equivocated, e.g., 'we are not sure of the Greek,' 'there is a parallel in the mystery cults to this,' 'this is a piece of Judean tradition,' 'this is but Paul's imagination,' or, 'this is a churchly interpolation.' Then, in the midst of our equivocations, God speaks: Let there be light! Immediately this creaturely equivocation ceases; unbelief burns itself out in a moment; and there before the eyes of our hearts stands

Jesus Christ giving the light of the knowledge of the glory of God on his blessed face (v. 6).[19]

One other major text that bears especially upon the issues involved here is Matthew 16:17. Jesus had asked his disciples who men said that he was, and they had reported a variety of opinions. When he asked them, "Who do you say I am?" Peter spoke for the group: "You are the Christ, the Son of the living God." Jesus' comment was, "Blessed are you, Simon son of Jonah, for this was not revealed to you by man, but by my Father in heaven." Although Peter and the disciples had seen and heard the same things that others had, their understanding had come by the Father's special manifestation of the truth.

3. There also are theological difficulties with Fuller's position. His view conflicts with other doctrines taught in the Bible, particularly the doctrine of total depravity, which holds that all persons are sinners both by nature and by choice, and that they are perverted throughout their natures. This doctrine does not mean that sinners are as sinful as they can possibly be, but that the perversion affects every aspect of their beings. It is not simply resident in their physical makeup, or their minds, or their wills. It has permeated their entire being, including the intellect.

This dimension of the doctrine is taught in a number of places in Scripture, and in a variety of ways. Jesus, for example, answered the disciples' query about his use of parables by saying that this was a fulfillment of the words of Isaiah 6:9–10: "You will be ever hearing but never understanding; you will be ever seeing but never perceiving. For this people's heart has become calloused; they hardly hear with their ears, and they have closed their eyes" (Matt. 13:14–15). Paul speaks of those who, although they knew God, neither glorified him as God nor gave thanks to him. Consequently, "their thinking became futile and their foolish hearts were darkened" (Rom. 1:21). He goes on to comment that "They exchanged the truth of God for a lie" (v. 25). Later in the same book he speaks of their stubbornness and

19. Bernard Ramm, *The Witness of the Spirit: An Essay on the Contemporary Relevance of the Internal Witness of the Holy Spirit* (Grand Rapids: Eerdmans, 1959), pp. 43–44.

unrepentant hearts (2:5), and says of Israel that "God gave them a spirit of stupor, eyes so that they could not see and ears so that they could not hear, to this very day" (11:8).

This picture of the unbeliever's condition seems definitely in contradiction to Fuller's view, which maintains that the natural man is, if skilled in the science of exegesis, quite able to understand correctly the meaning of the biblical text. He is able to do this as well as a regenerate exegete can. Indeed, he is able to see the truth even more than some believers, for, not holding that it is true and thus binding upon him, he does not experience any conflict between its teaching and his own tendency to self-glorification.

It would appear that we have here a case of what should properly be termed "epistemological Pelagianism." Sin affects humans, but not their ability to know. That ability, so far as we can determine, is undisturbed by the presence of sin in the unbeliever's life. With respect to that aspect of human experience, Fuller's view is the same as that of Pelagians. Sin affects the will, but not the reason or the mind. In those cases where the will does not conflict with the truth (because the mind does not regard the Bible as true and therefore its teachings are no threat), the ability to understand is not affected. It is only in those cases where the will conflicts with the Bible, that the will leads the reason to distort the teaching so that there is no real conflict. Thus, the effect of sin on the mind or the reason is only indirect. The Bible, however, clearly indicates that the mind or reason is negatively affected.

4. Fuller's stance is also faulty psychologically, as it separates the mind from the direct effects of sin. Underlying this view is a faculty psychology, which divides the person into intellect, emotions, and will. This faculty psychology is only implicit in the thought of Fuller, but it does definitely seem to be presupposed by all that he says. In the thought of Alfred Glenn, it is made explicit. Glenn explains the locus of depravity as being the will rather than the mind; the will, however, affects the ability to know.[20] It is not that the human cannot know, but rather

20. Alfred A. Glenn, "A Worthy Successor," *The Standard* 74/1 (Jan. 1984): 51.

does not want to know.[21] Although that is not what Fuller says, it is a further development of the faculty psychology.

This view was, for a long time, a popular view. In more recent years, however, it has been largely abandoned in favor of a more holistic understanding of human nature. The human is seen to be a psychosomatic unity. We do not act as body, soul, and spirit, nor as intellect, emotions, and will. What we do, we do as individual personal entities.

Nor is Fuller's view really supported by biblical statements. Disregarding the issue of trichotomism, dichotomism, or monism, we do not find in the Bible any suggestion of different components of personality (rational, emotional, and volitional) that function independently of one another. What we do, we do as unified entities.

5. There are also logical problems in Fuller's view. He is concerned about views that advocate finding the meaning of a biblical text solely through a special communication from the Holy Spirit, independent of any exegetical activity. This type of view also frequently comes up with an interpretation that has little relationship to the literal or grammatical-historical sense of the passage. The growing popularity of charismatic movements has given Fuller what is probably a reasonable basis for concern.

Fuller seems to have overreacted, however, in completely eliminating any direct influence of the Holy Spirit in the interpretational process. Unregenerate persons in a sense have no need for the Holy Spirit to assist them in determining the meaning of a biblical passage. The only role the Spirit plays is countering the conflict between the meaning of the passage and the natural human tendency toward self-glorification. In so doing, Fuller has opposed to the statement, "All of the understanding of the passage is given by the Holy Spirit," the statement, "None of the understanding is given by the Holy Spirit." He has aligned a contrary against the statement, a universal negative (E statement) against a universal affirmation (A statement).

This measure would not have been necessary, however. A contradictory would have provided an equally adequate rebuttal of the statement. Thus, the statement, "Some of the under-

---

21. Alfred A. Glenn, *Taking Your Faith to Work: Twelve Practical Doctrines* (Grand Rapids: Baker, 1980), pp. 136–39.

standing is not given by the Holy Spirit," would equally well have rebutted the original statement. What Fuller has in effect done, is to combine a whole series of such statements into a universal negative statement, in the process ignoring any possible intermediate points between the universal positive and the universal negative positions.

Another logical difficulty with Fuller's position relates to his understanding of the nature of different interpretations. By selecting Origen and C. H. Mackintosh as examples of the spiritual interpretation of the Bible, Fuller sets himself in opposition to a view "that the words of the text can play no essential role in conveying its intended meaning."[22] Fuller thus assumes that if the words do not play the entire role, they cannot play any essential role. And that leads him to the assumption that another interpretation will be an essential difference. Fuller seems to ignore the possibility of the biblical distinction between two Greek words for "other." *Allos* is another of the same kind; *heteros* is another of a different kind, something qualitatively different. May there not be a biblical interpretation that is other than another, not in giving a conflicting alternative, but simply in giving a greater depth of understanding of the same basic meaning? This might be what the role of the Holy Spirit in illumination would be. Yet this possibility, which we will explore at greater length in the concluding portion of this chapter, does not really seem to be considered by Fuller. Because he selects as his opposition relatively extreme forms of "spiritual" interpretation, he concludes that the result of some direct illumination by the Holy Spirit would be an interpretation contradictory to that obtained by exegetical study. Perhaps the relationship between the understanding that the Holy Spirit gives through illumination and that obtained merely by exegesis is something like that between universal and particular affirmative statements. "All A is B" and "Some A is B" are not contradictory. They have somewhat different, but not fundamentally opposed, meanings. We will need to pursue this distinction at greater length, however.

There is another logical difficulty with Fuller's view, although it is more of a linguistic issue. Fuller seems to hold that the unbeliever is capable of understanding the meaning of the

22. Fuller, "Holy Spirit's Role," p. 190.

biblical text, so long as he does good exegetical work. The unbeliever, of course, does not believe the things that he finds in the Scripture. They are foolishness to him. Nonetheless, he and the believing exegete can labor alongside one another.

Fuller seems to be ignoring the question of whether there are any differences between the statements, "This is what the Bible says," and "This is what the Bible says, and it is true" (or, in the case of a narrative passage, "and it really happened"). Does the second statement mean the same as the first? Does it add anything to the meaning of the first?

How we answer this question will depend on our understanding of the nature of language, particularly of propositions and predication. What we mean when we say that the latter sentence adds something to the former may involve us in something like the Anselmian statement of the ontological problem, and Kant's criticism of it, if we feel that version 2 predicates something more of the subject of the proposition than does version 1. This issue may perhaps instead be approached (in some specific passages) as an issue of the genre of literature affirmed by the latter versus the former sentence. In either event, it appears to me that there is a difference between the meaning of the two sentences, and we ought to explore what that difference is.

It is this question that Fuller fails to ask. That he sees no real difference in meaning between the two statements seems apparent from the way in which he refers to the unbelieving exegete's understanding. He does not say that such an interpreter understands part of the meaning of the text, while the believing exegete understands more. He does not, conversely, suggest that the unbeliever understands as much as does the believer, all other things being equal. But his failure to draw the distinction raises doubts about whether he sees any real difference in what the two understand. He would probably say that both understand the same thing, but one believes it and the other does not. To use the terminology we introduced earlier, the signification is the same for both interpreters, but the significance is not. But are the statements, "Paul said this, and it has no bearing upon the life of the reader," and "Paul said this, and obedience to it is incumbent on the reader," the same? Is the significance part of the signification? Since it not only had signification but also was evidently intended by the author to have significance for his first readers, this distinction may not serve us well for this issue.

6. Fuller's view also involves an epistemological difficulty. The logical difficulty is a case of not combining, "Some of the understanding is not given by the Holy Spirit" with "Some of the understanding is given by the Holy Spirit." In other words, it seems difficult for Fuller to integrate into his method of exegesis any positive role of the Holy Spirit in giving understanding of the passage. He is obviously very apprehensive about any approach that would bypass hard exegetical work, and in the process also bypass the grammatical-historical meaning of the passage. The role he assigns to the Holy Spirit in all of this is a therapeutic or prophylactic role—largely negative. It is to effect a change (largely a matter of sanctification) in the exegete that will prevent the natural tendency toward self-glorification from causing him to distort the plain meaning of Scripture. This, however, does not really add any new power of understanding to the believing exegete. It enables him to do what the unbelieving exegete does. Fuller's view suggests that the process of knowing the meaning of the text is, except for this prophylactic work of the Holy Spirit, primarily a natural or virtually mechanical process. Fuller has not thought through the process of how we come to understanding.

7. Fuller's stance also runs into the metaphysical problem of how the natural and the supernatural are related. This question may be asked on several different levels with respect to the meaning of the biblical passage. It may be asked on the level of the events that are purportedly asserted to have occurred. If this appears to be what we would ordinarily call a miracle, did it occur? Could it have occurred? Our conception of the relationship of the supernatural to the natural will often influence our answer to that question. Bultmann, holding to a closed continuum, believes that violations of natural law could not occur, so these miracles must be legend or myth. Supernaturalists believe that the relationship of God to the created world is such that he can contravene natural laws, causing miracles. Events for which there is adequate historical evidence are therefore understood to have happened, even if their occurrence is contrary to the known laws of nature.

There is a second level, however: the process of reporting the content of Scripture, or of recording the revelation. Here we ask about what was involved in the writing of the biblical accounts. Second-level naturalists assume that the production of the biblical documents can be fully accounted for by explaining the natural forces contributing to this writing. Supernaturalists, on the other hand, hold to the possibility of divine inspiration of the writer that enables him (or her) to produce something not accounted for by a study of the traditions through which oral material went, or the conscious intent of the author to interpret the material for his audience. It may be that even some evangelical form-critical and redaction-critical discussions of the biblical text can fall into this, if the interpretation excludes any real role for supernatural inspiration. The question, "Why is this in the biblical text?" is an important one. The answers we give to that question will tell us a great deal about our metaphysics. Similarly, "What was the role of the Holy Spirit in the production of this passage?" will get at the issue from the opposite side.

There is also yet a third level: the relationship of the role of the natural and the supernatural in the interpretational process. What is the relationship between hard, objective, exegetical work, and the illuminating work of the Holy Spirit? A naturalist would assume that the meaning of a biblical passage can be obtained simply by applying the canons of interpretation used on any type of literature to the literature of the Bible. A supernaturalist would hold, however, that there is an understanding of the text that cannot be obtained simply through intellectual study, but which the Holy Spirit gives in illumination. This is related to the objective, scientific study of the Bible in much the same way that the supernatural working of God stands in relationship to natural laws in a miracle. It need not be a different meaning, but it goes beyond the understanding that the unaided person would discover. It is on this level that it appears to me that Fuller is a practical naturalist, or a functioning naturalist. This, then, is tertiary naturalism.

At this point, Fuller would most surely vigorously object, and seemingly with good grounds. After all, there is a very definite supernatural work of the Holy Spirit in the believing exegete, which imparts to him the humble and contrite spirit necessary to receive what the Bible teaches. Note, however, that this is a first-level, not a third-level issue. This is a question of sanctification. Fuller certainly believes that the Holy Spirit works a work of sanctification that no natural laws can account for. But on the third level, the ability to understand what may have been written by a biblical writer about sanctification, the Holy Spirit plays no direct role. The sanctified exegete may not have any essential advantage over the unbelieving exegete in terms of ability to understand the passage.

We have now come to the end of our analysis of Fuller's position regarding the role of the Holy Spirit, although the analysis could have been deeper and numerous additional observations could have been made. Some readers may feel that I have already chewed more than I have bitten off, but I believe we could demonstrate that these are implications of what Fuller has said. Such additional analysis and demonstration go beyond the scope of the present treatment. What we must do, however, it seems to me, is to offer some reasonable alternative to what Fuller has proposed.

I do not intend here to present the biblical and theological data establishing the doctrine of divine illumination. That has been done elsewhere.[23] What I propose to do instead is to analyze somewhat more closely the nature of this illuminating work, particularly as it relates to the work of scientific exegesis. To do that, however, we must develop a bit of the biblical doctrine of epistemology of spiritual matters, if we may use an expression such as that.

The Bible does not present a complete discussion of human nature, but of the human person in relationship to God. Both the Jews and the Greeks, together with many other cultural groups within humanity, use the eye and the ear as metaphors for the

---

23. See Millard J. Erickson, *Christian Theology* (Grand Rapids: Baker, 1986), pp. 247–51; Fred H. Klooster, "The Role of the Holy Spirit in the Hermeneutic Process: The Relationship of the Spirit's Illumination to Biblical Interpretation," in *Hermeneutics, Inerrancy and the Bible*, ed. Earl D. Radmacher and Robert D. Preus (Grand Rapids: Zondervan, 1984), pp. 451–72; J. Theodore Mueller, "The Holy Spirit and the Scriptures," in *Revelation and the Bible*, ed. Carl F. H. Henry (Grand Rapids: Baker, 1958), pp. 265–81; Kenneth S. Kantzer, "The Communication of Revelation," in *The Bible—The Living Word of Revelation*, ed. Merrill C. Tenney (Grand Rapids: Zondervan, 1968), pp. 77–80.

mind. Within the biblical description, three levels of meaning are distinguishable.

There is first the level of physical perception. Here the eyes and ears are understood as physical organs. At the next level there is cognition, where the eyes and ears represent organs of the soul. There is, however, also another level, beyond hearing and seeing with the senses and seeing and hearing with the mind. This third level is what seems to be the focus of passages such as Matthew 13:13–15 and Mark 8:18. There are expressions such as the eyes of the heart (Eph. 1:18), seeing God (Matt. 5:8; 1 John 3:6), seeing the kingdom of God (John 3:3), and spiritual hearing (John 5:24; 10:3; Rom. 10:17). There are references to the organs of such spiritual perception—the heart, the soul, the spirit, and the mind. Finally, the Bible also mentions the products of the activities of these spiritual organs, such as thoughts, meditations, and words. Ramm summarizes: *"there is an inward power, or ability, or faculty in man which is deeper than the ordinary cognitive powers.* That is why Scripture can speak of a hearing which does not hear, and a seeing which does not see. It is this inward power or ability which, when sound and whole, has *an intuitive power for recognizing God and his truth."*[24]

What I am suggesting, then, is that the role of the Holy Spirit is not to convey new information that is not in the biblical text. Rather, the Spirit gives insight or understanding of the meaning that is in the biblical text, although it may not always be possible to unpack that meaning fully using exegetical methodology. What I am suggesting here is parallel to that which Ian Ramsey said about religious language. He suggested that the role of religious language was to elicit discernment of meaning that was objectively present within the statements, but could not be fully explicated empirically.[25] We are speaking of insight that cannot be pointed out directly and discursively through exegetical endeavors alone, but which is nonetheless there. Perhaps some illustrations will help clarify what we are saying.

---

24. *Witness of the Spirit*, p. 36.
25. Ian T. Ramsey, *Religious Language: An Empirical Placing of Theological Phrases* (New York: Macmillan, 1957), pp. 19–30.

Anyone who has taken an intelligence test that involves seeing analogies knows that there are right and wrong answers, which cannot always be fully explained. A person either gets them, or does not get them. Insight into certain relationships goes beyond mere understanding of surface meaning. The same type of thing occurs in mathematics. It is not always possible to explain algebra in such a way that every student will automatically see the processes and conclusions. A teacher may stand before a class and say, "1, 4, 9." Some of the students will respond, "16, 25, 36." Those who do demonstrate that they have seen some meaning that was objectively present in the symbols, but which was not obviously or overtly present. They may, of course, have either of two insights, each of which would apply equally well. Their insight might be, "Each number in the series increases over the preceding number by an interval equal to the preceding interval, plus two," or, "The series consists of the squares of succeeding integers." Whether the students had grasped the latter would depend upon their ability to reply to the number "144" by saying, "169." In one sense, however, the difference between the students who reply correctly and those who remain puzzled is not because those responding correctly have some new information not contained in the original numbers, but because they have more insight into that information.

This analysis could be carried into other areas of life, including social relationships. Here, of course, the problem is more complex because of the large number of subjective factors. What a person means may not always be obvious to everyone who reads her words, or even to everyone who hears them, because there are many nonverbal factors, some of which will not be detected and understood even by direct observation. Insight into the meaning may not be objectively explainable or demonstrable, but there is an objective meaning, namely, that which the speaker intends (excluding for the moment the issue of unconscious or unintended communication).

Other areas of experience also come to mind. A magnifying glass or a telescope does not provide some information not present in the object or scene we observe, but makes it possible for us to see something that is already there. It is seldom, however, that what is discovered on this level of examination is really different in nature from, or contradictory to, what we would otherwise see. It is merely an elaboration, a more detailed form, of the other.

The role of the Holy Spirit in illumination, then, is to convey insight into the meaning of the text. Illumination does not involve the communication of new information, but a deeper understanding of the meaning that is there. It is the flash of understanding, which may come suddenly and dramatically or more gradually and quietly, but in which we come to see that which we had not previously understood. It is an experience like that described by Ramsey, in which "the ice breaks and the penny drops."[26] It is not something opposed to the careful study of the biblical text. In a sense, the Holy Spirit is able to work more effectively, the more objective knowledge one gains of the meaning of the vocabulary and syntax of the text, for he works through that information, not independently of it. His work is more like that of tutor than of a lecturer. It is seeing in a deeper sense and with that deeper level of perception that the Bible speaks of as seeing with the heart.

Does not this leave us open to a new subjectivity, however? How do we know that all have the same illuminated meaning, or how do we know which of several possible meanings that different interpreters find is correct? There are two important responses to this significant question. The first is that there is a dimension of intersubjectivity. Those who have seen the structure and solution to an algebra problem know that they have indeed arrived at the correct understanding. Others can agree upon that, although it cannot be proved using objective demonstration. Similarly, there will be insights that others can also come to see. The second response, however, relates to the fact that differing schools of thought seem to see different illuminated meanings. It should be noted, however, that the basic, and most crucial dimensions of Christian truth are considerably more direct and obviously on the surface of the text, so that honest and objective unbelievers can see them as well. As important as the deeper dimensions of understanding that come only through the illumination or enlightenment given by the Holy Spirit are, they are not essential to salvation or to Christian fellowship.

26. Ibid., p. 25.

3

Getting from There to Here

The Problem of Contemporization of the Biblical Message

Conscientious, concerned Christians have at some point in their lives recognized that God really is God, the creator and ruler of all that is. In the light of this realization, they have committed themselves to the Lord, and desire to live for him and to please him. They want to know what his will is for them, so that they may do it.

For evangelicals, the Bible is the authority for faith and practice. They understand the Bible to be God's revealed truth, preserved in written form as a result of the Holy Spirit's work of inspiring the writers, so that what they wrote faithfully preserved the revealed message, so that the written document actually is the Word of God. Thus, evangelicals or conservative Christians faithfully and diligently study the Bible, seeking to understand it, so that they can obey it.

The Problem of Contemporization

Here, however, we soon become perplexed. The Bible says that we are not to eat anything that swims in the water but does not have scales. Does that prohibit us from eating catfish, bullheads, or, for that matter, squid or eels? The Bible says that

55

women are not to cut their hair, and that men are not to have long hair. Is that injunction mandatory for believers today? The Bible says that women are to be silent in the church, and that they are not to teach. It also says that when someone strikes us on the cheek, we are to turn the other cheek for that person to strike also. It says that we are not to take a sword, but also that we are to take a sword. It records a command to wash the feet of others, as well as one to sell all we have and to give the proceeds to the poor. What are the implications of these biblical teachings for believers today? Are we to follow them, or have they become immaterial and irrelevant?

We are dealing here with what I have chosen to call the problem of getting from there to here: how to move from the message of the Bible in the time it was given to its message for today. In many ways, I think the issue of contemporizing the biblical message is possibly the single most important issue facing evangelical hermeneutics today. By this I mean simply the matter of how to faithfully preserve the meaning of the biblical message in its context, while applying it to the present time in a contemporary form.

This is a problem that all segments of the church struggle with. It is in a sense more acute for evangelicalism, however, because as a conservative movement, it strongly desires to ensure that it not alter the basic biblical message. Its task has been made even more tense in recent years as a result of intensified efforts to make sure that its message is truly speaking to the present age. Two indications of this concern are contemporary Bible translations (actually paraphrases—especially *The Cottonpatch Bible* and *The Living Bible*) and the emphasis of a growing number of churches on contemporary worship services, particularly those geared to the needs and interests of non-Christians, so-called seeker services being the most highly developed form.

This attempt within evangelicalism is not going completely smoothly, however. One indication of this is the objection by many conservative biblical scholars to the paraphrastic translations. Some years ago, I served as an editor for an encyclopedia that was being produced by the publisher of *The Living Bible*. I telephoned one scholar at an evangelical seminary that prided itself on being avant garde and definitely not fundamentalistic, to ask him to write a particular article. He asked about the relationship of the encyclopedia to *The Living Bible*, and then, without waiting for an answer, launched into a tirade against *The Living Bible*. "I and my colleague, Dr. X," he said, "are going everywhere we can, warning everyone about that translation." Although I was tempted to ask, "Haven't you stopped burning Bibles yet?" I simply thanked him for his thoughts and assigned the article to someone else. While extreme in degree, the attitude was not unique among evangelicals. On the other hand, some of the ministries that are the most successful in making their message appealing to today's young people are not very careful about their exegesis of the biblical texts. What is needed is some clear thinking about how we can make the transition from the biblical text to the present situation. Yet, as Alan Johnson has pointed out, evangelicals are (or were in 1982) just beginning to say the first words on this subject.[1]

William Hordern makes an important distinction between translators and transformers.[2] Both groups attempt to state the Christian message in a form that is intelligible to a person functioning within contemporary culture. The transformer, however, believes that such radical changes have taken place in the world that some of Christianity's basic conceptions are simply no longer tenable. Consequently, the transformer is prepared to abandon certain of these tenets to modernize the message. The translator, on the other hand, is intent upon retaining the essential message, but stating it in a form that will make sense to a thoroughly modern person.

Varieties of the Difficulty

My commitment is to the translator, rather than the transformer, approach. It is essential for a conservative to preserve the integrity of the Christian world- and life-view. For most conservatives or evangelicals, the alternative to the translator

1. Alan F. Johnson, "A Response to Problems of Normativeness in Scripture: Cultural versus Permanent," in *Hermeneutics, Inerrancy, and the Bible*, ed. Earl D. Radmacher and Robert D. Preus (Grand Rapids: Zondervan, 1984), p. 230.

2. William E. Hordern, *New Directions in Theology Today*, vol. 1, *Introduction* (Philadelphia: Westminster, 1966), pp. 136–54.

approach is not that of the transformer, but rather what we might term the "nondialogical" approach. This view simply states the biblical message in the same language and thought forms of the Bible. The necessity of translation, in the sense given above, is made apparent, however, by a number of issues.

1. The first of these is the simple fact that there are a number of biblical statements regarding situations for which no parallel exists today. An example is the large amount of material devoted to prohibitions of practices associated with Baal worship. Baal worship is, to my knowledge, no longer extant today. This fact would seem to render a fairly significant body of biblical material irrelevant to us.

2. A second type of consideration is present-day situations on which the Bible apparently makes no statements. How to treat AIDS patients, for example, is never addressed, nor is there any discussion of abortion per se. Here again, the Bible appears to be irrelevant.

3. Another type of issue presenting difficulty is when the biblical writer addresses a specific situation superficially similar but actually quite different from that which we have today, and perhaps in significant ways. Thus, women today still have hair, which may be worn at different lengths, but something about 1 Corinthians 11:3–16 hints that perhaps the teaching does not apply in that form universally.

4. A further indication of some difficulty with unmodified application is where there is contradiction between this particular teaching and some other teaching apparently addressing the same issue. An example would be Luke 22:36, where Jesus tells his disciples to acquire a sword, and Matthew 26:52, uttered just a few hours later, where he warns against the use of the sword. More relevant morally would be passages like Genesis 9:6, where the taking of human life is prohibited but also commanded.

5. Finally, there are passages that seem to conflict with general revelation. A prime example was the church's idea that the Bible required belief that the earth was flat, which resulted in the Copernican revolution.

In actuality, we should be diligent in attempting to determine the underlying intent of the passage or the signification within the signification, even where none of these problems is evident. Otherwise, we are simply assuming that the Bible is speaking in an absolute or universal fashion whenever we do not have reason to believe otherwise. That is the position of someone like J. Robertson McQuilken, who writes, "My thesis of a fully authoritative Bible means that every teaching in Scripture is limited unless Scripture itself treats it as universal."[3]

Signification and Significance

We need to note, however, that the issue is not merely as simple as applying past teaching to present situations. That conception has been encouraged by a number of factors, not the least of which has been the terminology introduced by Hirsch. Hirsch distinguishes between what he calls meaning and significance. Meaning is that which the author intended by what he wrote, the truth he was attempting to convey. Significance, on the other hand, is the relationship of those symbols to a person.[4] Thus, the distinction tends to be meaning = content intended then; significance = application now.

There are two problems with this set of categories. The first has to do with the terminology itself. The word "meaning" is applied to what is really just part of a broader understanding of meaning. In addition, "meaning" is in popular usage often identified with the latter term or significance, as in a statement such as, "That really has meaning for me."

I would like to suggest a pair of terms that I believe would be more precise. Meaning will be the inclusive term, of which the two subdivisions are signification and significance. These are roughly equivalent to Hirsch's meaning and significance, respectively, but not precisely so. Signification is the dimension of meaning with respect to the relationship between a sign or term and that which it signifies. Significance refers to the dimension of meaning with respect to the relationship between the sign and someone knowing it. This may be either someone

---

3. J. Robertson McQuilken, "Problems of Normativeness in Scripture: Cultural versus Permanent," in *Hermeneutics, Inerrancy, and the Bible*, ed. Earl D. Radmacher and Robert D. Preus (Grand Rapids: Zondervan, 1984), p. 230.

4. E. D. Hirsch, Jr., *Validity in Interpretation* (New Haven: Yale University Press, 1967), p. 8.

at the time of the writing of the passage or someone reading it many years or even centuries later. This distinction is very similar to that drawn by Charles Morris between the semantic dimension of meaning (the relationship of the sign to its referent) and the pragmatic dimension of meaning (the relationship between the sign and a knower).[5]

Does the signification of a statement ever change, after the author has written or the speaker has spoken it? In one sense, this is a moot point. The meaning cannot change. It has been fixed in the statement by its originator. Its meaning comes from there. It is not contributed to or affected by the receptor. In another sense, however, the meaning does change, for the statement may well have been directed to someone in a specific contextualized situation. When a receptor is in a different situation, the meaning may be different.

Let me offer an illustration. Suppose a speaker is describing a particular object. He says, "It is three feet to your left." Suppose, however, I move five feet to my left. What is the signification now of the speaker's statement? We might say that the signification is still the same, but the truth-status has changed. It is no longer a true statement. Yet in another sense, the signification has changed. Now it is, "It is three feet left of where you used to be." This is not really a question of significance, for the receptor is being treated objectively, that is, as a reference point for the location of an object, rather than subjectively, that is, in terms of the implications of the statement for one. That this is true can be seen by substituting someone else for oneself, as in the statement "The object is three feet to his left," or, "The object is three feet left of where he used to be." It can be perhaps even more clearly seen with inanimate objects, such as in the statement "The knight is one space to the left of the pawn," or, "The knight is one space to the right of where the pawn used to be." The signification of the statement has changed, because the referent of the statement was not merely an object, but in a real sense, a relationship. When that relationship changes, the signification of the statement changes.

5. Charles W. Morris, *Foundations of the Theory of Signs* (Chicago: University of Chicago Press, 1938), pp. 1–9.

What this shows us is that there is a sort of "signification be-hind the signification," or a "timeless, unrestricted, universal signification," as it were. The form of that is, "The object is three feet left of where he was at that time," or, to safeguard against movement of the object, even without the intervention of a human agent, as by the wind blowing the object, "The object was three feet to the left of him." The signification of that statement will never change, or become untrue. It will always be the case that the object was at that point in time three feet left of where he was at that time.

Nor is this necessarily a matter of shift or change on the part of the receptor. It may be the change that occurs in the signification when a shift is made from one receptor to another. If A's original statement to B is, "The object is three feet to your left," then the signification to C, who stands five feet to B's left, can-not be, "The object is three feet to your left," for the object is ac-tually two feet to his right. It must rather be either, "The object is three feet to B's left," or, "A said to B, 'The object is three feet to your left.'" The latter statement, however, really has a differ-ent meaning than the original statement, for it is now a state-ment about that statement, rather than another version of the statement itself.

Now let us take another type of example, involving temporal rather than spatial issues. Suppose we take the statement, "The temple will be destroyed." That statement had a fairly clear sig-nification prior to A.D. 70. What, however, is the signification of that statement now? Either it is "The temple will be destroyed," in which case it is false, or, "The temple has been destroyed," which seems to be a different statement. There is another possi-bility, however: that the signification for us of the writer's state-ment, when written, was, "The temple will have been destroyed." It may be preferable to say, "From the perspective of the first hearers, the signification was, 'The temple will be de-stroyed.'" It appears that prophecies are a somewhat unique type of statement with respect to signification.

It should be noted that the dimension known as significance cannot be made merely a question of time. A passage has signif-icance for readers today. It also, however, had significance for the first readers, the readers at the time of the writing. These significances may be quite different, however. This may be because there actually is a difference in the signification. For example, for someone living in the time of one of the prophets, the prophecy regarding the captivity of the nation of Israel would have the signification, "Israel will be taken off into captivity." It certainly does not have that signification for us today, however. The event has already taken place. Just what that signification is, and the relationship of it to the signification when originally written, is an issue that necessitates considerable reflection.

Just what is the nature of this difference? Haddon Robinson suggests that we must determine the meaning intended by the biblical writer for those of his time as well as later, which he identifies as the theological purpose, without specifying whether this is one meaning or two.[6] We may begin our inquiry into the question of the meaning (in both senses) for then and the meaning for now, by examining the nature of meaning in narrative passages.

Let us take as an example the narrative in Genesis 22, in which Jehovah commands Abraham to take his son Isaac up to Mount Moriah and offer him as a sacrifice. The signification seems to be the same both for persons at the time of the writing and for us: God commanded Abraham to offer his son. What is the significance of this passage for us today, however? Not that we are to offer our children as sacrifices to God. That would be a literal or noncontextualized, or what I would term, "legalistic" use of the Bible. The same would be true of the idea that God will provide a substitutionary sacrifice, as he did for Abraham.

Two-Step and Three-Step Hermeneutics

What is usually done in this type of case is to say something like, "The message to us today is that we should be willing to give to God what is most precious to us, whether that demand our willingness to let him take our child through illness, or our willingness to let him call one of our children to foreign missionary service, or our willingness to give up our house, car, savings and investments, or whatever."

6. Haddon Robinson, *Biblical Preaching: The Development and Delivery of Expository Messages* (Grand Rapids: Baker, 1980), p. 93.

A fairly common hermeneutical device in many evangelical circles is to take the biblical teaching and apply it directly to the situation today, by finding its meaning for today. A. Berkeley Mickelsen, for example, speaks of the difference between exegesis and exposition, quoting with apparent approval the view of James Smart on this subject. He says, "There are two steps involved. First, we must discover the meaning of the expression or statement in the past. Then we must drive this meaning home to our present society with the same impact it had when it was originally written."[7]

Whether in ethics or theology, however, the aim is not simply to repeat the same words. It is not merely when we translate one language into another that this is an issue. Even within a given language (although some might question whether it is still really the same language) we cannot merely repeat the same words. Words change meaning with the passage of time. That is one of the problems with using the King James or Authorized Version of the Bible today. The meanings of words like "ghost" and "Spirit" now are reversed, and a word like "prevent," used to translate 1 Thessalonians 4:15, meant "precede" in 1611 but now means "hinder." (I once dealt with a rabid advocate of the use of the King James Version who failed to understand this, and actually thought that 1 Thessalonians was teaching that those alive will not hinder the resurrection of those who have died in the faith.)

What we need to do instead is to enable the words to have the same impact on us that they were intended to have on the first hearers or readers. We need to interpret what Paul said to the Corinthians so that we will hear what Paul would say if he were writing to us today instead of to the Corinthians. This is similar to what Charles Kraft has termed a "dynamic equivalent." We must endeavor in Bible translation *to be faithful both to the original author and message and to the intended impact that that message was to have upon the original hearers.*[8] Accord-

7. A. Berkeley Mickelsen, *Interpreting the Bible* (Grand Rapids: Eerdmans, 1963), p. 56.

8. Charles H. Kraft, *Christianity in Culture: A Study in Dynamic Biblical Theologizing in Cross-Cultural Perspective* (Maryknoll, N.Y.: Orbis, 1979), pp. 270–71.

ing to Kraft, to preserve the content of the message, we may need to alter the form.[9] In actuality, I would prefer to put it, utilizing terms previously introduced, as preserving "the signification behind the signification."

Isolating the Time Factor

The problem, however, is to determine the present-day equivalent of that earlier meaning. We need to ascertain the common element between the two statements. If AF is the statement as originally written and AG is the meaning for today, then what is A? To put it differently, what is the permanent or timeless element or independent variable that is carried over from one situation and time to the other? Here I would suggest that this timeless meaning of Genesis 22 is something like, "God expects us to place him ahead of all other objects of value for us," or, "God always provides or enables us to do that which he requires of us."

Some might suggest that this is the original signification of the text, but that, strictly speaking, is not so. The signification is simply, "God commanded Abraham to sacrifice his son Isaac," and, "God provided a sacrificial animal to Abraham." To make that more general statement the signification of the passage is to slip an additional step into the first step. What is needed, before stating the meaning for today, is to identify the meaning for all time. A three-step, rather than a two-step, hermeneutic, is required.

Sometimes the task of identifying the universal factors as opposed to the local or restricted factors is thought of in terms of which rules are unrestricted and which are restricted. This is sometimes put in terms of permanence of norms. It is not, however, a matter of deciding which rules are universal and which are not. It is a matter of recognizing the locus of normativity as being the principle that underlies the command, and noting that some principles can only result in one rule regardless of context, whereas the implications, application, or result of other principles may be quite varied.

9. Ibid., p. 273.

This timeless truth will be seen to be a principle, rather general in nature, as contrasted with specific statements of meaning. It is not, however, as vague as the most general principles, such as love and justice. It was limitation of normativity to only one general principle, love, which lay at the root of Joseph Fletcher's situation ethics.[10] The same type of danger can also infect our hermeneutics. It is this that McQuilken fears in Kraft's dynamic equivalence: that it will become possible to justify virtually anything on the basis of finding only rather general principles.[11] Instead, as John Goldingay has pointed out, it will be the intermediate level principles, which in many ways resemble what ethicists like to call "middle axioms," which are operative here.[12] I would suggest that one reasonable limitation on the method be that we look for principles of the maximum degree of specificity that meet the criteria for generalizability. This is a policy generally followed in preaching as well, where we could otherwise take such general lessons from a passage that many sermons would be virtually identical, save for the specifics of particular passages.

Criteria for Identifying Principles

But how do we arrive at these principles, or how do we determine the permanent meaning of the passage? While this principlizing approach is fairly widely advocated, often relatively little is done by way of suggesting how to identify the principle.[13] Others have offered some suggestions. Goldingay proposes four criteria:

10. Joseph Fletcher, *Situation Ethics* (Philadelphia: Westminster, 1966), pp. 57–68.
11. McQuilken, "Problems of Normativeness in Scripture," pp. 224–25.
12. John Goldingay, *Approaches to Old Testament Interpretation* (Downers Grove, Ill.: InterVarsity, 1981), p. 55.
13. See, for example, the virtual absence of discussion of criteria for identifying principles, in Walter Kaiser, *Toward an Exegetical Theology: Biblical Exegesis for Preaching and Teaching* (Grand Rapids: Baker, 1981), pp. 151–63. A similarly brief treatment is given in Robinson, *Biblical Preaching*, pp. 92–93. For an overview of the method of "principlizing," see Ebbie C. Smith, "Ten Commandments in Today's Permissive Society: A Principleist Approach," *Southwestern Journal of Theology* 20/1 (Fall 1977): 42–58.

1. Examining a statement in the light of comparable ones where the principle may be more overt.
2. Considering the statement in the light of parallel extra-biblical materials.
3. Examining the statement in the light of the overall biblical message.
4. Finding the theology that "undergirds" or "informs" the actual text.[14]

Terrance Tiessen, dealing with the problem of identifying universal moral absolutes, proposes the following criteria for universal norms:

1. Basis in the moral nature of God.
2. Basis in the creation order.
3. Transcendent factors in the situation of their promulgation and the lack of situational limitation in their formulation.
4. Consistency throughout the progressive revelation of the divine will.
5. Consistency with the progress of God's redemptive purpose.[15]

Elsewhere I have proposed the following criteria for permanent elements in revelation:

1. Constancy across cultures.
2. Universal setting.
3. A recognized permanent factor as a base.
4. Indissoluble link with an experience regarded as essential.
5. Final position within progressive revelation.[16]

---

14. Goldingay, *Approaches to Old Testament Interpretation*, p. 54.

15. Terrance Tiessen, "Toward a Hermeneutic for Discerning Universal Moral Absolutes and Applying Them in Contemporary Contexts," unpublished paper presented at the annual meeting of the Evangelical Theological Society, New Orleans, Nov. 15, 1990.

16. Millard J. Erickson, *Christian Theology* (Grand Rapids: Baker, 1986), pp. 120–24. See also *Relativism in Contemporary Christian Ethics* (Grand Rapids: Baker, 1974), pp. 138–39.

A major factor will be to look for the underlying reason that makes this meaning valid. If we ask of the statement, "God commanded Abraham to sacrifice his son, Isaac," "Why?" the answer will be, "Because he is the only true God, deserving of the full commitment of his creatures." If we ask, "Why?" regarding the statement, "God provided Abraham a sacrificial substitute for his son Isaac," the answer will be, "Because of the faithfulness of God" (who had, after all, promised Abraham this heir).

Note, also, that the emerging answer is doctrinal. What makes specific or contingent events occur, and occur in the way in which they do, is always some aspect of theology, frequently of the doctrine of God himself.

This insight, that the factor of permanence in narrative passages is theological, has been recognized by a number of hermeneuts. One of these is Haddon Robinson, who maintains that "application must come from the theological purpose of the biblical writer."[17] Similarly, John Bright says that "the preacher needs to understand not only what the text says, but those theological concerns that caused it to be said, and said as it was said. His exegetical labors are, therefore, not complete until he has grasped the text's theological intention."[18]

This suggests that a crucial step in the interpretation of the Bible today must be performed by the third segment of the theological curriculum and theological faculties. It is not uncommon for the discussion to be carried on somewhat like this: "Biblical scholars decide what the meaning of the Bible is, and the practical departments, especially preaching, apply that message to today." This may represent a certain amount of imperialism on the part of biblical scholars. In any event, the role of the historical scholars, in helping determine the nature of changes that have taken place in culture with the passage of years, and of theology, in helping identify the essential doctrinal elements, needs to be reaffirmed.

In preaching, these doctrinal principles will constitute the basis, or the main points, of our sermons. Thus, the sermon will not speak of Abraham in its basic thesis or proposition or in its

17. Robinson, *Biblical Preaching*, p. 91.
18. John Bright, *The Authority of the Old Testament* (Nashville: Abingdon, 1967), pp. 171–72.

major points. Rather, it will speak of God, the timeless one. Similarly, the aim of systematic theology is to draw out the theological content of Scripture and to state that content in a timeless form. Although it will also be expressed in an idiom appropriate to the setting, the major goal is to state it apart from these restrictions.

It is important to bear in mind that the biblical passages were written to definite audiences at definite times and places. In other words, the expression of the message is already contextualized. It is therefore not enough to determine just what was said in the biblical passage. We must determine the lasting or uncontextualized version of that message. The biblical expression is superior to any later expression, because the former is God's immediate revelation. It is not necessarily superior, however, to what the message would have been had it come to a different time and situation. It would, of course, have been different, for it would have been differently contextualized.

We should note that there are two aspects to this temporal contextualization. There are what we might term roughly ethical statements in Scripture. These ethical statements pertain to the way in which people are to live, how they are to conduct themselves. These statements, of course, are frequently contextualized. There are also some seemingly permanent or universal ethical statements. One of these is the prohibition of murder in Genesis 9:6. There the definite impression is that no one, ever or anywhere, is to commit murder. What underlie these imperative statements are indicative statements, statements about what is right and wrong or good and bad. These, in turn, are derived from theological statements about how some things are, such as what God is like, or what the nature of the human is, and thus, what is good for a human being.

One problem is how we are to move from discussions of local situations to their universal basis. This might be called the ethical problem, or the problem of ethics (as contrasted with a moral problem, or a problem of morals). There is a second problem, which we might term the theological problem or the problem of theology. Even when the Bible discusses these permanent or universal issues, it is still directing its message to people in one time and place, and hence is using the language that makes sense to them. So Paul, for example, in the Book of Romans discusses timeless theological truths, such as sin and justification. He is, however, discussing these truths with the Christians in Rome at about the middle of the first century. Consequently, the problem of theology is to determine how much of the discussion dealing with timeless topics is timeless, or is the essence or the content, and how much is the form of expression to those people. Frequently the problem is to determine what is part of the doctrine, and what is a metaphor intended to clarify the doctrinal truth.[19]

The aim, then, of interpretation, is not simply to reproduce the biblical statement and apply it to the present. It is rather to decontextualize that statement, to remove all the elements related to the unique situation, and then find an appropriate form for expressing this statement in a different situation and to a later time.

When we come to the type of biblical material that we will broadly term ethical, we find a somewhat different situation. Here there is sometimes a difference between the signification of the time of writing and that of the present time (or any other time subsequent to the biblical setting). Part of this problem lies in the fact that the statements are in a different mood—the imperative (or some variation of it), rather than the indicative.

We must now ask further how we can identify the timeless elements of content, as contrasted with the specific forms of expression at a particular time and place. On the one hand, we do not want to require of Christians that they hold to a localized expression of faith and practice. We do not want to insist that anyone today become a first-century A.D. Corinthian in order to be a good Christian. On the other hand, we do not want to dismiss as culturally displaced some belief or practice that is part of the permanent essence of Christianity.

We have noted that one way of identifying the underlying principle is to ask "Why?" or to seek to determine the reason or basis for an action or teaching. Beyond this, however, we need to attempt to establish whether this principle does indeed ap-

19. For an example of a treatment of a specific doctrine using this method, see Millard J. Erickson, "Principles, Permanence, and Future Divine Judgment," *Journal of the Evangelical Theological Society* 28/3 (Sept. 1985): 317–25.

pear in Scripture beyond the limitations of a given time and place. Here we find more help than we may have expected. The Bible was written by a variety of authors, at an assortment of times and places, to very different audiences. Thus we may be able to obtain from a comparative study some indication that we are dealing with a universally applicable principle. This, then, is the next question to ask: Where and under what conditions does teaching regarding this matter appear in the Bible? Is it found only in one setting, or across a variety of settings?

One teaching that we might take as a test case to which to apply this principle is the biblical practice of tithing. Tithing was taught and practiced throughout the Old Testament. Was it simply part of the Old Testament way, or is it of permanent applicability? Here it is helpful to note that the general principle of proportionate giving is part of Paul's teaching in 1 Corinthians 16:2. Jesus told the Pharisees that they ought to have practiced tithing (Matt. 23:23). Thus it appears that tithing is one of the permanent elements in Christianity.

Quite different, however, are the dietary and sanitary regulations of the Old Testament. These practices were followed almost exclusively by the Hebrews during the Old Testament period. There seem to be no parallel practices in the New Testament. While this in itself does not mean that we are dealing with a restricted principle, we have no assurance that we are not.

Another question we need to ask is whether the reason for a given biblical teaching is no longer valid, or if it is, if this teaching or action is now obviated because of a different and better way of fulfillment. An instance of the former is the command to proliferate in Genesis 1:28. God told Adam and Eve to be fruitful and multiply, to fill the earth. The reason, in this context, is apparent. It was so that they might have dominion over the whole of creation. Being few in number, and lacking any type of mechanization or automation, they could only carry out God's mandate by a considerable and rapid multiplication of their numbers.

Does this command still apply to us? Is it necessary for all humans today to marry and reproduce, and to the maximum possible extent? Here we must ask, "Why?" And the response is, "In order to fill the earth, to be able to exercise dominion over it." But is this reason still valid? The signification of the statement, being a narrative passage, is unchanged. "God said to man, 'Be fruitful and multiply and fill the earth, and have dominion over it'" is still its signification. But while it is still necessary for humans to exercise dominion over the earth, that mandated task no longer requires a large population, given modern technology. It appears that the command to be fruitful and multiply and fill the earth has been fulfilled sufficiently. Indeed, if anything, this command seems to have been fulfilled excessively. Thus, the reason for it, at least to the degree originally proposed, no longer exists.

Somewhat different are the healing narratives found throughout the Bible. Since they are found in all parts of the Bible, we might conclude that we are here dealing with a universal or absolute factor. The signification of each passage is basically similar—that God miraculously healed (Sarah, Naaman, the centurion's servant, etc.). If we raise the question, "Why?" the answer in each case seems to be something like, "Because, as a loving and merciful God, he does not desire to see his children suffer."

This principle presumably is still valid and in effect, since God does not change. We must ask, however, whether that principle and that characteristic of God still call for that action. We might note, for example, the tremendous progress that has been made in medicine since biblical times. Many conditions that formerly could only be cured miraculously now are routinely cured by medical treatment, often on an outpatient basis. But if we believe in general revelation and divine providence, then healing through medical science is as much God's doing as is a miracle.

There is another question to be asked, however. The answer to the question, "Why?" may not be sufficient, for our loving God heals not just to show compassion, to relieve the suffering of his children. It may also be to bring glory to himself. This would seem to be a reason for continued miraculous healing. It should be noted, of course, that the glory given to God is likely to be greater in those instances in which medical science has not shown itself capable of healing than in those in which it has.

There is another consideration bearing on this specific matter, however. In Matthew 4, we have an account of Satan's temptations at the beginning of Jesus' public ministry. Satan attempted to induce Jesus to cast himself down from the temple pinnacle, since God would send his angels to protect Jesus. Jesus' reply was a word of rebuke: "You shall not tempt the Lord your God." Apparently, requiring an unnecessary display of God's power is wrong, because by so doing we attempt to dictate to God what he must do. We thereby usurp his place and his authority.

God's revelation is progressive. For example, the Old Testament involved a sacrificial system. We must ask whether that is a permanent factor, that is, whether the signification is, "God *provides* atonement for human sin through the sacrificial system," and is true for now as well as then, or, "God *provided* atonement for human sin through the sacrificial system." The New Testament revelation regarding the atoning death of Christ suggests that it is the latter rather than the former. It is clear that Christ's death has supplanted the sacrificial system. This would seem to argue that the permanent factor is an underlying principle something like: "God provides for human salvation through a vicarious, substitutionary atonement."

But if this is the case, do we have any justification for absolutizing the atonement in Christ? Is it not just another contextualized form of the general principle? If not, how can we be sure of the general principle? If we cannot, how can we be sure that we have not simply absolutized some other teaching for which we have no later versions of the principle?

The distinct feature of Christ's atoning death is the way it is described and interpreted by other biblical texts. There is a finality about it; it completes the process. The need for divinely provided, substitutionary atonement for human sin has been met, once and for all.

Treatment of Apparent Contradictions

We now need to examine a different kind of case, one in which we encounter a teaching contradicted by or at least contrasted with, two or more other instances in Scripture. These cases have played a large part in ethical discussions. Fletcher in fact made this a major consideration in his argument for situation ethics: moral laws cannot be absolute or universal, because two or more conflict.[20] Although he was dealing with claimed moral laws, from whatever source, the issue applies just as strongly to biblical affirmations, and perhaps especially to them, since these purportedly are divinely revealed and hence the more absolute. It is, however, not merely ethical commands that display these apparent contradictions. Other declarative statements, claiming to reveal how God is, and even historical statements, sometimes conflict.

One way to look at these seemingly contradictory statements is to regard them as complementary, rather than contradictory. This involves saying that each states correctly an important part of the truth, but *only* a part. For example, proverbs can often be paired against one another, such as "Answer a fool according to his folly," and "Do not answer a fool according to his folly." Another example would be "Too many cooks spoil the soup," and "Many hands make light work." In other words, there are some situations in which several persons in the same kitchen would be desirable, and others in which this would create a problem. So also there are times when we should, and other times when we should not, answer a fool.

In some cases, it may be that these are different contextualizations of the same principle. Applying a given principle in one culture may require the exact opposite action that would be appropriate in another culture. Because the actions or the proverbs deal with at least similar issues, it makes sense to look closely for the possibility of a common principle being applied to different situations.

A second possibility is that these cases are instances of two different principles. Both principles are further illuminated when we see the application of each.

A third possibility is that more than one principle bears upon this situation. In one case there may be the principle common to the two cases, plus another principle that applies. In another case, there may be the common principle, plus a different principle or principle(s), different than the variable principles in the first case. This is often true of ethical situations, which are

20. Fletcher, *Situation Ethics,* p. 36.

frequently quite complex. When applied, the resultant rule may be quite involved.

This situation points up the necessity of systematic theology being involved in the principlizing process. Otherwise we will end up working with several principles, any one of which we might be inclined to absolutize. We will then have conflicting absolutes. Even with respect to the signification of a statement, it will be necessary to do an inductive study of the whole of Scripture, to make certain we have not unduly absolutized a particular form of understanding.

There is, of course, a way around this dilemma. It is Kaiser's contention that a passage can only be interpreted in the light of preceding revelation. In a qualified sense, this is most certainly true.[21] Yet when Kaiser moves to principlizing the precept or specific historical occurrence, he may be giving an inadequate or incomplete principlization of that specific. Or he may have principlized an interpretation of a nonfinal statement. Thus it would seem that the type of biblical theology that we need cannot be restricted to understanding a passage in light of only itself and earlier passages. It cannot be the theology of Genesis, or even of the Old Testament alone, which is used to ascertain what is going to be preached in what form. It will have to be systematic biblical theology.

It will also be helpful to engage in comparative study of parallel passages. Here is where redaction criticism is of special value. The Gospel writers were doing the very thing that we are talking about here: contextualizing the message to the audience to which each was writing. To be sure, the amount of variation was relatively small, for each Gospel writer was dealing with specific teachings of Jesus. Yet they were taking what they perceived (or were led by the Holy Spirit to identify) as the essence of what Jesus had said, and expressing and applying it to specific audiences. What we will preach, then, to our audience, will not be Matthew's, Mark's, or Luke's message, but the message of Jesus that lay behind each of these Gospels, as applied to the situation of our own audience. It will be instructive for us to see how each of these evangelists contextualized that message.

21. Kaiser, *Toward an Exegetical Theology*, pp. 134–40.

Two final observations need to be made. First, we need to be certain that we clearly distance ourselves from the biblical situation before we attempt to apply it to our own situation. This distancing will ensure that we do not too easily make a transition from the biblical situation to our own. We will need to engage in as careful and thorough an exegesis of the contemporary situation as we do of the biblical context. Only then will we be able to find an appropriate parallel in the present to the text we are trying to apply to it.

Second, we have been thinking primarily about the movement from there to here. In reality, however, we frequently find ourselves starting from here, and going there (to the biblical text), in order to move back here again. What about those cases in which we are faced with a contemporary issue to which the Bible does not seem to offer any specific guidance, or which it does not specifically address?

The Need for Principlizing the Present Situation

Here we need to principlize the current situation as well. It is only then that we can ascertain what within the biblical revelation might bear on our action. For example, we might take the issue of drinking alcoholic beverages, specifically total abstinence. Those who use the Bible in a legalistic fashion sometimes say that the Bible in no sense supports abstinence, since it nowhere commends or commands that practice. If anything, the Bible recommends moderation in the use of alcoholic beverages. The issue is not as simple as that, however. For in biblical times, there was no danger that someone whose peripheral vision and reflexes were diminished because of the use of alcohol would cause a serious traffic accident. The worst that might happen would be that he would run his donkey or his camel into a tree, although since these animals have sight and sense, which an automobile does not have, such an accident would be unlikely to occur. There were no high-powered automobiles or freeways then. What the Bible does present quite clearly is the prohibition of taking another human life, especially when this is intentional, but also when it results from negligence. That is one of the major issues associated with drinking. For long before a person has become intoxicated, there is impairment of abilities. In fact, the Federal Aviation Administration will not allow a pilot to fly an aircraft eight hours after the consumption of any alcohol, and most airlines prohibit their pilots from drinking any alcohol for twenty-four hours before flying. Here, principally, is the relevance of Scripture to the issue at hand.

Today's social problems associated with alcohol were not present in biblical times. Intoxication was less common. For one thing, the modern methods of distillation were not available. For another, it was common, in New Testament times, to dilute wine with anywhere from one to twenty parts of water.[22] Nor was alcoholism apparently the large-scale problem that it is today in the United States, where, statistics tell us, one out of every ten persons who takes the first drink will end up as an alcoholic. Here the biblical principle of not causing one's brother to stumble (1 Cor. 8:13) is applicable. Although there is a 90 percent probability that the Christian can take a drink without harming himself and without directly harming anyone else, taking that drink may cause someone else to begin drinking, and there is a 10 percent probability that *he* will become an alcoholic.

I have been a total abstainer for as long as I can remember, but the real depth and force of that conviction did not come to me experientially in church or Sunday school or from studying the Bible. The conviction came upon me forcibly while I was on my knees in a grubby apartment on the near northwest side of Chicago one night when I was a young pastor there. I listened to the tearful prayer of Mr. Wilson (not his actual name), a prayer I had heard this alcoholic pray many times before. Yet his drinking problem had returned again and again, and I had made several trips with his wife and two children to a family shelter. That night I prayed a prayer, too. I said, "Lord, I promise you that I will never do anything that might lead anyone to come to the state of affairs that this man is in."

The Bible is a strong source of guidance, perhaps more so than we have realized. It may take hard work to utilize it in some cases, but the results are worth the effort.

---

22. Robert H. Stein, "Wine-Drinking in New Testament Times," *Christianity Today* 19/19 (June 20, 1975): 9.

4

The Contributions of Church History, Theology, and Cross-Cultural Studies to the Hermeneutical Task

We have noted, in an earlier chapter, the tendency of the biblical and the practical disciplines of the theological enterprise to divide the work of hermeneutics between them.[1] Initially, with hermeneutics focused on the past dimension, on determining what a given passage of Scripture meant when written, the labor was conducted almost exclusively by Old and New Testament scholars. Hermeneutics, in other words, was basically reducible to exegesis, and that, everyone agreed, was the domain of the biblical specialists. Later, with the broadening of the understanding of hermeneutics to include application to our present-day situation, those engaged in teaching the practice of ministry, especially preaching, gave special attention to how that biblical content should be given relevant contemporary expression. They were the custodians of the tools needed for understanding present-day culture.

1. Walter C. Kaiser, *Toward an Exegetical Theology: Biblical Exegesis for Preaching and Teaching* (Grand Rapids: Baker, 1981), p. 21.

In all of this, one group of laborers in the theological vineyard seemed to stand unemployed and perhaps unemployable: the church historians; theologians, including both systematic theologians and philosophers of religion; and students of cross-cultural studies. This was unfortunate, not simply because these people were left out, like persons not invited to a party or chosen to play in a game, and thus felt neglected, unwanted, and useless. Rather, a valuable resource was being neglected, a resource that we now recognize is indispensable to the task of hermeneutics in the broadest sense. For if the biblical scholars possessed the ability to understand the biblical message in its context and the practical theologians comprehended the thinking and language of the present time, then the historians, philosophers, and theologians are in the best position to assist us in relating the former to the latter. To vary the imagery: biblical scholars are experts in the source of spiritual vitality, the generator as it were; the practical theologians are experts in the expression or implementation of the faith, the motor of the present time; the historians, theologians, and cross-cultural specialists are experts in the wiring that connects the two, the past and present, the Bible and Christian life and ministry, the generator and the motor. Thus, in the original imagery, at the eleventh hour these laborers have also been pressed into service in the vineyard.

The Hermeneutical Contributions of Church History

What, then, are the roles that these disciplines can especially perform? I would contend that they are in a position to fulfill the tasks uniquely required for hermeneutics in our time. We will begin by enumerating the hermeneutical functions of the historical discipline.

1. Its first function is to identify the historical variations of expression or application. Sometimes when we approach a given statement, its meaning seems obvious, virtually self-evident. Yet there may be many possible ways of interpreting and applying it. If we fail to see this, we may succumb to the temptation of absolutizing the relative, of making one *possible* interpretation the permanent essence of the teaching or command.

One way of discovering the possible interpretations is to see what interpretations have actually been held. This procedure is somewhat similar to the way sidewalks are laid out on a new college campus. When the campus is constructed, the sidewalks are not immediately put in. The landscape architects first observe the traffic flow, where students actually walk, and then lay the sidewalks there. The same, of course, applies to other building complexes besides academic campuses. I have sometimes advised committees formulating a new policy that if they want to learn every possible interpretation of that policy they have only to publish it and wait. Sooner or later, every conceivable interpretation (and even some inconceivable ones) will be articulated by those who want their interpretation to govern their particular case.

We have the benefit of nineteen centuries of church history, during which persons have reflected on various passages of Scripture. Out of their study and thought have come a multitude of interpretations, theories, doctrines, and hypotheses. These will help make us aware of the richness of meaning that may or may not lie within the Scriptures. It is not then a matter of taking the lowest common denominator and making that the essence. The task is not that simple, but at least a beginning has been made in determining the possible variations of expression of the biblical statements. Some of those expressions may have been appropriate and adequate for their day, others not.

In particular, I believe that we in the conservative or evangelical segment of Christianity have failed to learn enough from the early centuries of church history. Instead of examining the original contextualizations of particular types, we have instead relied on contextualizations of contextualizations. We sometimes have been critical of earlier theologians because they are so far removed from our situation and used categories that to us appear to be foreign to the biblical material. We forget, however, that many of them stood much closer to the original biblical situations than we do, and in many cases, stood in an intellectual heritage much more like that of the biblical writers than is ours. We should not automatically assume that we understand the biblical writers better than the fathers did. This sort of intellectual snobbery assumes that what is later in time is necessarily better.

2. Another function of the historical discipline is to teach us how cultural factors affect the expression of a doctrine. One function of church history is not simply to tell us what happened, but to attempt to show us why it happened. Thus, for example, the particular form that the doctrine of the atonement took reflected what was perceived to be the major need at the time. In a period of ethical laxity, the example theory had special appeal; at a time when the power of Satan and evil was considered quite formidable, the ransom (or, as Gustaf Aulen has termed it, the "classic") theory of the atonement was the most appealing. Conversely, of course, there were contrasting theories that assimilated these tendencies, rather than opposing them. With a rich and multifaceted doctrine such as this, the facet of the doctrine that comes in for special attention reflects, as it should, the situation of the times.

History does not necessarily repeat itself or move in cyclical fashion. There are, however, similarities and approximations to earlier periods. By noting the similarities between our period and others in church history and observing which nuances of expression of a doctrine were especially effective at that time, we may gain a clue to the most adequate interpretation to be used at the present.

3. Church history can also teach us something about the science and art of contextualization. Certain disciplines can be learned deductively; others must be learned inductively. Many invoke a combination of these approaches, including contextualization. A number of rules or guidelines on how to decontextualize or find the permanent essence or the enduring principles of a doctrine have been offered by different practitioners of hermeneutics. Some have articulated rules regarding how to recontextualize. Not all of this can be learned in didactic fashion, however.

Frequently those who are the most effective practitioners of a given skill cannot explain how they do it. They either possess this ability intuitively, like musicians who play "by ear," or they have so assimilated the methodology that they are no longer conscious of the steps that they go through in executing that action, like experienced drivers driving an automobile. One study was done in which a medical student followed a famous diagnostician on rounds for several days, observing as he made his medical diagnoses, which were generally accurate. When asked, however, how he knew that a particular condition was an instance of a particular disease, the diagnostician frequently replied that he simply did not know how he had arrived at that specific conclusion.

Likewise, many of the most important theologians in the history of the church did not write discourses on theological methodology. They simply proceeded to do theology, correlating their statements with the pressing issues and thought forms of their day. We can learn a great deal about theological contextualization by reading Augustine's *City of God* or Martin Luther's *Babylonian Captivity of the Church*. These men and many other theologians were master contextualizers. Just as we may learn an art better by observing how an artist performs it than by listening to his discourse about it, so we can gain much by reading the theological works of great theologians, when those are seen in their historical context.

4. The study of church history can also help us recognize the historical conditioning and hence historical relativity of our own theological formulations. Every attempt to interpret the Bible is from within a given, historically conditioned situation. The way we perceive the biblical truth is affected by our viewpoint. What we can see is a result of where we stand, of our perspective on things. Yet frequently our limited perspective is not apparent to us; we think we have seen the whole of the matter, or we unconsciously fill in the blanks from the portion that we do have. I recall in particular a discussion in an epistemology class in which the instructor placed an orange on the table, and then asked us what we saw. Several members of the class said that they saw an orange, but the instructor reminded them that at most they saw only the front half of an orange. The class eventually divided into two groups: those who said, "I seem to see an orange," and those who said, "I have an orange-colored, elliptical sense datum." It was a vivid reminder that we often do not see all that we think we see. We frequently supply the rest. We are often, in some ways, like the five blind men confronted by the elephant. We tend to think that the whole of the truth is synonymous with what we have seen.

What is true of spatial perspective is also true of historical perspective. We can see something at one point in history that we cannot see at another point. As we look back on the history of the church and Christian thought, it is fairly easy for us, especially when quite a distance removed in time, to see the limitations of others' perspectives, to observe that they failed to see certain things in the text because of their historical blinders.

What is not so easy to see is the limitations of our own historical perspective. We have a tendency to identify how we see things, not with our perspective, but with *how things are*. Awareness of the historical conditionedness of other viewpoints should sensitize us to the fact that every view within history has similar limitations.

I was once involved in a conference of Christian scholars that included primarily sociologists, plus a few philosophers and theologians. One theologian presented a paper that dealt with a particular formulation of one doctrine by a theological school of a hundred years ago, which he identified as "the old Princeton theory," and related it to the Scottish commonsense realistic philosophy that was popular at that time, which he believed formed the philosophical basis leading these theologians to their particular interpretation and synthesis. When he finished, another theologian asked him, "A century from now, when historians discuss the old _____ theory (naming his institution), what will they say *its* philosophical presuppositions were?" It was as if the question had been asked in Japanese or some other unfamiliar language. He simply could not comprehend the question. The sociologists present, however, saw the issue immediately.

The study of the history of interpretation should help us see that our interpretation is not the final view, some position held independent of and from beyond history. It should encourage us to look for our own presuppositions and hold our interpretations with a certain amount of tentativeness and humility. We will be likelier to heed the exhortation, "Bethink thyself that thou mayest be wrong!"

5. Finally, the historical discipline should enable us better to evaluate a view by helping us see the implications of similar

views. It is not always possible to verify a specific interpretation of a passage directly on a point-for-point basis. We simply do not have that direct confirmation, either through correspondence with data in the passage or empirical experience. What then is sometimes done is to draw out the implications of the interpretation of a passage, thus giving us a broader synthesis, easier to confirm or disconfirm, since it gives more potential points of reference.

One form that this endeavor sometimes takes is to draw out the implications of this possible interpretation and other possible interpretations, and then see which of these fits more harmoniously with other teachings (or the implications of other teachings) that are quite clearly and definitely presented in Scripture. Sometimes these implications are not immediately seen, and not by the person first propounding the interpretation. The process of discovering these implications can be slow and painful.

In some cases, however, the study of church history enables us to accelerate that process. If, for example, we are considering an interpretation of John 14:28, to the effect that Jesus really was inferior in essence to the Father, we need not wait to discover the implications. We may look at the interpretation of the passage made by Arianism some sixteen centuries ago. To the extent that the two historical interpretations are members of the same genus, we can conclude some things about the implications and thus also the truth of our interpretation by examining its ancient counterpart.

The Hermeneutical Contributions of Theology

We now must examine the role that theology, especially that variety usually referred to as systematic theology, plays in hermeneutics.

1. First, theology provides the abiding or permanent element from biblical statements—the essence that we accordingly carry over from the biblical form of expression to the present time. As we noted in Chapter 3, often we cannot simply apply the biblical statement to our present situation in direct or unmodified fashion. This is because matters of historical narrative have a

particularity about them. We are not Abraham, Jonah, or Jairus. We do not live in Hebron, Bethlehem, or Philippi. Many of the Bible's propositions, because they are historical, describe what happened to someone else at a specific time and place, and hence do not apply directly to us. Similarly, imperative statements in Scripture frequently refer to circumstances quite unlike our present experience, and thus are not directly applicable.

We seek for the bridging factor, asking, "God did this in biblical times. What does God do in our time?" or, "God said this in biblical times. What does he say in our times?" We seek the basis of God's actions and statements at all times. God does not speak or act arbitrarily. Our doctrine of God helps us understand why he acts as he does. Historically, there have been two major theories regarding this. Nominalism maintains that God is totally free, arbitrary, spontaneous in his decisions. He can choose to act differently than he does, even to the extent of lying or breaking his promises. Realism, on the other hand, holds that God is bound by external principles or laws. He cannot choose other than the right, which exists externally to him.

Neither of these views appears to me to fairly represent the biblical revelation. God's actions are not arbitrary. He cannot, for example, lie or break his word (Heb. 6:18). He cannot choose different moral behavior than he does. This, however, is not because of some external moral standard, superior to him, to which he must conform his behavior. He does what he does because of who he is. There is an objective standard of right and wrong, but it is not external to his nature. It is the very way he is. His command to his believers and followers to act in certain ways is because he is of that very same character himself (e.g., Lev. 11:44–45). Logically antecedent, then, to God's actions and his commands is his nature, which does not change throughout time (Mal. 3:6; James 1:17).

This means that the task of identifying the permanent element in the passage we are interpreting is a theological task. Once we determine that God did or said what the Scripture reports, we will then have a basis for seeking to determine its application to the present time.

Note, however, that this is either a function of systematic theology, or of the type of biblical theology that Brevard Childs recommends: biblical theology of the canonical type.[2] It will not do simply to attempt to generalize the specific passage and apply it to the nature of God. We may not find enough in this passage about God and his nature to be able to define that nature in a well-rounded fashion, or to know exactly what attribute is involved. For that we will need to consult the fuller understanding of God, drawn from the entire biblical revelation.

This may seem to some to be a case of eisegesis, of reading in meaning from elsewhere. Even if this is a seemingly commendable use of other portions of Scripture, it is still eisegesis, and therefore illegitimate. Note, however, that this is not the first hermeneutical step and therefore not truly exegesis. It is the second step of the hermeneutical method. It is not claiming that this is what the text says, but that this is the underlying basis of the text and of the interpretation thereof.

We have spoken primarily of doctrine as it pertains to the nature and actions of God, or theology proper. It pertains equally, however, to other doctrines, which are also timeless truths. So when the issue is the nature of humanity, atonement, or the church, we must also seek for these timeless components or bases of support for the declarative and imperative sentences of a given passage of the Bible.

2. A second role of theology is closely related to the first one: it gives us inclusive teaching on a subject that will help us avoid absolutizing any one particularized or contextualized form of teaching about that subject.

As we have noted several times in this volume, many of the writings contained in the Bible are occasional in nature, being addressed to definite times and places and with definite audiences in mind. To those settings they are conveyed with a tone of real absoluteness. Yet the form of expression often reflects a one-sided situation. That, for example, is why we find such differing emphases in Galatians and in James. Biblical theology alone, however, might restrict itself to one of those expressions, and thus we might absolutize a partial statement to the neglect of the remainder of the truth.

2. Brevard Childs, *Biblical Theology in Crisis* (Philadelphia: Westminster, 1970), pp. 149–219.

This is not to say that the message of the passage is to be other than that affirmed there. It does mean, however, that we will be careful when we preach and teach. We must strive to match the aspect of the truth in a passage to the situation. For example, we should not take a passage written to an antinomian audience and use it as a sermon text for a group of legalistic hearers, at least not with the same degree of emphasis. We must always bear in mind the other facets of the truth, and make the application of this aspect while holding it in tension with the others.

3. Systematic theology also serves the function of analyzing the real meaning of the concepts asserted and discussed in the biblical text. This is one of the primary steps in theological methodology, and one that theology performs in the hermeneutical endeavor.

Analysis has always played a significant role in theology. We can find it, for example, in the scholastic method exhibited in Thomas's *Summa*. There it takes the form of a statement of a position, followed by an objection and then a reply to the objection. It is a means by which the theologian progressively refines the meaning of what he is saying, by eliminating some possible meanings and elaborating on others.

More recently, theology has utilized the methods of analytical philosophy, especially of the ordinary language variety. Here the approach is to press relentlessly the question, "What do you *really* mean by that?" As applied to biblical statements, for example, this approach poses at ever deeper levels questions such as, "What does 'born again' mean?" "What does reconciliation refer to?" "What is being described by union with Christ in the Bible?" Note that what we are engaged in is *theological* interpretation of biblical concepts.

The early form of analytical philosophy, logical positivism, developed a principle of meaningfulness called the verification principle. This principle held that the meaning of a synthetic proposition was the set of sense data that would verify or falsify that proposition.[3] It eventually became apparent that this prin-

3. Rudolf Carnap, "The Rejection of Metaphysics," reprinted in *The Age of Analysis: 20th Century Philosophers*, ed. Morton White (New York: Mentor, 1955), pp. 209–12.

ciple was too narrow, because on its own criteria, the principle itself was meaningless. The difficulty came in the restriction of verification to sensory experience. There is, nonetheless, a point to this principle, namely, that a statement that is consistent with absolutely any state of affairs is meaningless. If we cannot specify what would count against the truth of the statement, then, of course, nothing really counts for it. It possesses what one of my graduate professors termed an "infinite coefficient of elasticity of words." These verbal symbols can be stretched indefinitely without breaking. It is the task of theology, as informed by linguistic philosophy and other disciplines, to ask what would count against this assertion, and thus help to determine what this really means.

The meaning asserted by the biblical author is of prime importance. Sometimes, however, the author raises more questions than he answers, and gives us little real basis for inferring more. Here is where a number of practices must be brought to bear. Some of these will be drawn from general revelation. Knowledge of the created world, of the nature of persons, language, and relationship will enter in. These will be somewhat generic concepts. What is being done here is parallel to what archeology does for our understanding of culture, history, and geography. It is also parallel to the use of various kinds of critical methodology to get at the meaning of the biblical text. If that is not eisegesis, then this surely is not either.

The sources drawn upon will vary: anthropology, linguistics, psychology, sociology, and many other disciplines. We must always be careful, however, to make sure that no distorting presuppositions are introduced through this channel. Bearing in mind that sin does affect our ability to know the truth accurately, and that this effect is inversely proportional to the distance of the doctrine from the center of Christian faith, namely, the relationship between God and the human,[4] we will be vigilant in excluding humanistic or naturalistic elements. We must constantly compare the substance, methodology, and presuppositions of the "secular" discipline to the express statements of Scripture.

4. H. Emil Brunner, *Revelation and Reason* (Philadelphia: Westminster, 1946), p. 383.

4. Theology also contributes to the accurate interpretation of Scripture by helping us identify presuppositions of the interpretational method and of ourselves. To some extent, this issue has been addressed under the contributions of history, but theology also gives attention to this endeavor, in perhaps an even more intense fashion. The first step is simply to become aware that, like all other persons, we have presuppositions or assumptions.

Our presuppositions will color what meaning we find in the passage we are investigating. Presuppositions are like spectacles. We view the biblical text through them. While some interpreters proceed as if biblical interpretation is an ideologically sterile procedure, unaffected by any predispositions or preunderstanding, that is an ideal that probably is never reached, although we should certainly strive to approximate that ideal as closely as possible.[5] These presuppositions are of various kinds and function at many different levels. Some are logical, some philosophical, some linguistic, some theological.

How do we go about identifying presuppositions in ourselves and in others? A first step is to acquire a broad acquaintance with the culture within which we are working. A thorough liberal arts and theological education kept current by widespread, continued reading is crucial. This will help us recognize influences that are at work.

We will also endeavor to recognize our own presuppositions. This may be done in several ways. One is to submit our thought to scrutiny by those of different viewpoints, seeking to obtain their interpretation of our assumptions. I have long advocated theological self-understanding groups, much like the psychological self-understanding groups that were so popular in seminaries a decade or so ago and still continue in somewhat diminished capacity. In such a group, each person would share a significant theological conviction or a crucial experience, and would then be given feedback by his or her peers.

Such feedback will help us compensate for our natural biases. As a Baptist, for example, I must require more evidence than appears to me to be necessary for interpretations that sup-

5. James Leo Garrett, Jr., *Systematic Theology: Biblical, Historical, and Evangelical* (Grand Rapids: Eerdmans, 1990), 1:ix.

port that view. The same would also be true for a Calvinist or an Arminian with respect to seemingly favorable interpretations. It is a matter of trying to compensate consciously for the biases we know we hold.[6]

We must also be critical of the presuppositions of authorities we consult. If this is not done, errors and distortions are built in from the very beginning. This means that before relying too strongly on a commentary, theological dictionary article, or lexicon, we should seek to determine something of the background and convictions of the author. James Barr, for example, has pointed out the biases of the mighty *Theological Dictionary of the New Testament*.[7] It may not be necessary to make a compensation, and it would not be wise to do so in an exclusive fashion, since the author may have already done that, and additional compensation would result in overcompensation. We should, however, be alert to this and should scrutinize the writing especially carefully.

5. A further function of theology is to help evaluate the methodology of biblical interpretation. For one thing, we need to determine carefully what constitutes verification of an interpretation as correct. In any science, the methodology requires some statement about what constitutes proof.

What usually is done in interpreting a passage is to offer an explanation of its meaning. Then there are generally observations or reasons offered, supporting this theory or showing how it fits the data of the passage. Sometimes the alternative or competing interpretations are also stated, together with critical comments on them.

What is really needed, however, is some measure of the likelihood of the theory presented. This cannot be done in some quantitatively precise fashion, as with the natural sciences or mathematics. What is disconcerting, however, is that the reader often has difficulty assessing whether the probability of this interpretation has been established.

6. Millard J. Erickson, *Christian Theology* (Grand Rapids: Baker, 1986), p. 57.

7. James Barr, *Semantics of Biblical Language* (New York: Oxford University Press, 1961), pp. 206–62.

Perhaps what is needed is a healthy dose of inductive logic, as is used in the scientific endeavors to establish the truth of a theory. We should consider how many possible interpretations there are, and the major strengths and weaknesses of each hypothesis.

In particular, theology will want to evaluate the methodology of biblical criticism. In recent years, cracks have begun to appear in the once uniform trust in these methodologies. In particular, the presence of numerous subjective factors has become apparent. The form-critical application of some of the criteria of authenticity to the Gospels has not resulted in uniform agreement regarding the results.

It should be possible to test the validity of some of the tenets of biblical criticism. There are recent documents to which the methodology could be applied, then checked by consulting some of the persons involved, including the author. This would allow modification and refinement of the method. The difficulty, as C. S. Lewis once pointed out, is that Saint Mark is not alive and therefore cannot protest the interpretations of his writing.[8] Lewis himself once wrote a particular piece that was then analyzed and evaluated by a reviewer. The reviewer thought he saw signs in the writing that indicated that Lewis was not very interested in what he was doing at the time. In reality, however, the exact opposite was the case.[9]

6. Theology also assists us by tracing out the implications of a given interpretation of a passage. One of the ways of finding out what something means is to find out what is contained within it, which is really what implication is. Sometimes this may turn out to be quite different, and even contrary, to what seems on the surface of it to be the case.

Part of the implication issue is the effect that the adoption of a given interpretation, as opposed to another one, has on other doctrines, of which it is one of the premises. The meaning of this portion of Scripture must be seen in light of the larger universe of theological discourse.

8. C. S. Lewis, "Modern Theology and Biblical Criticism," in C. S. Lewis, *Christian Reflections*, ed. Walter Hooper (Grand Rapids: Eerdmans, 1967), p. 161.
9. Ibid., p. 159.

7. An additional role that theology plays will be in the analysis of the arguments employed in interpretation of the Bible.[10] Frequently, the case for a given interpretation rests on rather loosely defined argumentation. It is not readily possible to assess the truth of the interpretation, since the logic cannot be tested. The statement being presented may appear quite plausible.

Plausibility alone is not enough, however. Unless we hold to relativity or plurality of truth, there cannot be innumerable contradictory interpretations, although there may be degrees of adequacy of the several views. If we can identify the form of the argument, its validity can more easily be tested. To the extent that theology concerns itself with these overarching ideological issues of truth-testing, it can be of help to us here. It may show, for example, that the argument is actually a case of undistributed middle term, and thus invalid, or that what is an argument from analogy is actually an illustration of the truth rather than a proof of it. Analyzing the argument also allows it to be put into a more generic class, so that its probability can be assessed in a more objective fashion, removed from the emotional or nonrational factors that may apply to the specific issue under discussion.

We also need to ask about the logical connection of the verse or phrase under consideration and its immediate context. It is common to insist on the need to interpret within context, appealing to slogans such as, "A text without a context is a pretext." It is not sufficient, however, to ask what the context is. It is also necessary to ask about the nature of the relationship of the text to that context. Is it one of inclusion within an earlier (or in summation, later) statement? Is it an illustration of that principle? Is it compared or contrasted with the other statement? Are the two enumerated as instances of yet some larger class, which may even be unnamed or unstated?

Failure to ask such questions may lead to serious misunderstandings of a text. An example is James Nelson's discussion of homosexuality. He deals with the prohibition of homosexuality

---

10. D. A. Carson is to be commended for his chapter on logical fallacies in *Exegetical Fallacies* (Grand Rapids: Baker, 1984). This type of analysis needs to be an essential part of all exegetical endeavor.

in Leviticus 18 and 20 by claiming that the context is the prohibition of Canaanite fertility worship, then stating that it was because that worship involved sacral prostitution and orgies that it was wrong, rather than being wrong in itself.[11] Another example is Clark Pinnock's interpretation of Acts 4:12, in which he claims that salvation includes healing (Peter and John were called before the Sanhedrin to account for the healing of a crippled beggar). He says, "Peter tells us that physical healing is part of salvation."[12] He fails to ask, however, about the relationship of the healing of the one man to the salvation of the 5,000 and the real referent of Peter's use of the term "salvation." In both of these cases, we appear to have a logical connection assumed rather than argued, supporting a conclusion previously arrived at on experiential grounds.

Frequently, what is most needed is to lay bare the structure of the argument. For when closely examined, the argument will often be seen to be an enthymeme, that is, an argument containing suppressed premises. Because they are assumed rather than being brought to light and scrutinized, the relative plausibility of the premises is not explored. When, however, they can be tested, the validity of the syllogism that underlies the hermeneutical conclusion can be more carefully evaluated.

Craig Blomberg's article, "Degrees of Reward in the Kingdom of Heaven?" gives us several excellent examples of suppressed premises or unrecognized assumptions, which affect his exegetical conclusions. For example, he says: "A final logical question could be asked: If the heavenly aspect of eternal life represents perfection, is it not fundamentally self-contradictory to speak of degrees of perfection? Surely theologians ought to reconsider a doctrine that involves an elementary lexical and conceptual fallacy."[13] The unstated assumption, however, appears to be that perfection must be the same in all individuals. If that is the case, however, are we not led to the conclusion that

11. James Nelson, "Homosexuality and the Church," *Christianity and Culture* 37/5 (April 4, 1977): 64.

12. Clark Pinnock, "Acts 4:12—No Other Name Under Heaven," in *Through No Fault of Their Own? The Fate of Those Who Have Never Heard,* ed. William V. Crockett and James G. Sigountos (Grand Rapids: Baker, 1991), pp. 108–9.

13. Craig L. Blomberg, "Degrees of Reward in the Kingdom of Heaven?" *Journal of the Evangelical Theological Society* 35/2 (June 1992): 162–63.

if redeemed believers are perfect in heaven and God is perfect in heaven, then what the believer will undergo must be deification, rather than glorification? The alternative, of course, which Blomberg does not consider, is that perfection is relative to that which is perfected. We will not necessarily all be identical personalities in heaven. There will be a perfection of the unique status of the individual as possessed at the end of life. Blomberg also says, "Not surprisingly—but nevertheless tragically—the spirit of competition, comparison with one another, and rewards on the basis of merit have overwhelmed many aspects of Christian living as well, both corporately and personally."[14] Here the assumption appears to be that pursuit of rewards is competitive, that receiving rewards must be at the expense of another believer. But where do we find that God "grades on the curve," as it were? This assumption, plus another, stated but unsupported, that there cannot be both differences of reward and lack of awareness of the differences, also leads him to see an alternative, noncompetitive view of degrees of reward, as containing an "unwitting contradiction."[15] A final example is his assumption that rewards necessarily work against true grace by becoming the motivation for faithful service.[16] But is this so? In the parable of the talents, the master did not promise any reward at all. Yet, the reward was given, regardless. In other words, rewards may come as a surprise, just as "the first shall be last" and "whoever loses his life will find it." This, of course, may not be a correct alternative assumption, but the point is that the assumptions must be argued, rather than simply assumed. Numerous other such unstated assumptions appear in Blomberg's article, serving as suppressed premises. These then lead him to rather strained exegesis, to virtual psychoanalysis of the opposite position. These also lead him to find inconsistencies in the thought of those who differ with him.[17] Since he fails to recognize that these are assumptions, he does not realize that others might be working with different assumptions, so he

14. Ibid., p. 169.
15. Ibid., p. 162.
16. Ibid., pp. 169–70.
17. Ibid., p. 162.

finds inconsistencies within their thought, whereas the inconsistency is between their thought and his.

8. Another way theology assists us is by placing the interpretation in a genuinely systematic context. It allows us, causes us, forces us, to relate the teaching derived from this particular interpretation to other teachings of Scripture, some of which may well be more clearly and definitely taught than are others.

Often it is not possible to assess the truth, or to determine the meaning, of a given proposition in Scripture, by taking that proposition in isolation. It is, however, when we spin out the implications of a statement, and thus generate a larger web of propositions, that we can more adequately assess these dimensions of the meaning. For one thing, this gives us more points of contact with the data (in this case, the data of the Bible).

The other way in which this endeavor works is in bringing the implications of the interpretations that we are considering into contact with other teachings supported by the Bible. Truth, including especially biblical and theological truth, is organic in character. Thus, one part of the truth cannot conflict with another part. So although we may not be able to test directly an interpretation under consideration, we may test it indirectly, by tracing out implications. For example, our interpretation of a given verse may be A. Let us say that A implies B, for which we may have only tenuous or ambiguous biblical support. Suppose, however, that proposition X is clearly taught by Scripture, and that it implies Y, which in turn contradicts B. This requires that we reject interpretation A, in favor of A' or something of that type. While agreement of the implications of the two propositions does not confirm A, but only contributes to its probability in the fashion of inductive logic, the contradiction of the two certainly works to refute A.

Pinnock's interpretation of Acts 4:12 might have been improved if he had asked some questions about this interpretation in relationship to other considerations, both inside and outside the passage. So, for example, he might have asked why no mention is made of other healings among those 5,000 persons. Were there no other persons in need of healing in a group of this size? If so, were they not healed, but instead simply left in their condition? Or was this simply omission of reference? If so, why was that done, if this indeed is holistic salvation? Should that not have been made clearer, if that is indeed an aspect of salvation? Further, if salvation really is inherently holistic, should not all Christians be free from illness? And if this is part of salvation, how can it be that God does not in every case grant the request for healing, whereas he never denies the request for forgiveness of sins and new birth? Do these sick Christians lack the perfect faith possessed by Christians who are well? What about other physical provisions? Should the passages about miraculous feeding not be interpreted in such a way as to support the wealth portion of the "health, wealth, and happiness" formula, in the way in which this passage is found to support the health portion? And since Pinnock goes so far as to apparently endorse the idea that healing is found in the atonement, based on this passage, he should also ask about the innumerable issues that doctrine raises.[18]

The Hermeneutical Contributions of Cross-Cultural Studies

There is a third discipline that needs especially to be brought to bear upon the work of hermeneutics. It is the field of cross-cultural studies, whether that be taught in the department of communication, or as more commonly is the case, in the department of missions. This discipline concerns itself with the communication of the message and the establishment of the practice of Christianity in varying cultures. It has a number of contributions to make to our task of interpreting the gospel.

1. This discipline can serve much the same function for us geographically that history serves for us temporally. If history has the value of being able to show us insights into a text, or even the methods of interpretation that have varied with the passage of time, then cross-cultural studies can do the same thing laterally.

All of us are, to varying degrees, captives of our own cultures, and of the presuppositions resulting from that location and orientation. This limits what we find within the text, for a differing perspective is frequently required in order to see other aspects

---

18. "Acts 4:12," p. 109, n. 6.

of the truth. Contact with other cultures and with Christians from these other cultures can supplement the limited perspective that we might bring to the endeavor.

Those who have ministered in other cultures can testify to this phenomenon. One of my colleagues recently experienced this in discussing the biblical story of Joseph with some African Christians. North American Christians find in this passage evidence of God's providence, Joseph's faithfulness, and similar themes. The African Christians, however, saw family ties in the passage. Despite all that Joseph's brothers had done to him, he did not take revenge on them, but included them in the benefits that had come to him. The ties of blood were much stronger than circumstances. Although Joseph now spoke Egyptian and held the second most powerful position in the nation of Egypt, he was still basically Hebrew.

Contact with other cultures enlarges our understanding of the text. It enables us to see facets of the truth to which we are blind because of our cultural limitations. It does not give a different meaning to the text, but a fuller meaning. And it does not say that the text has different meanings for different persons— a sort of epistemological subjectivism. But it reminds us that there are meanings in the text that are meanings for everyone, but that some persons may be more likely to observe certain of these meanings than are others, simply because of their perspective on things.

To some, who emphasize the single meaning or single intent of Scripture, this may seem to be a case of eisegesis, of reading in something that is not present within the text. I would prefer to think of it instead as the removal of exegetical blockage, of the negation of the sort of blindness that our situation in time and space sometimes seems to consign us to.

This is not to say that the insights presented by those with a different perspective are simply to be accepted as valid, without any question about their genuineness. They must be scrutinized carefully, to make certain that they are genuinely there, rather than being the importation of the assumptions of their advocates.

2. Cross-cultural studies also help make us aware of flaws in our own thinking. We have noted earlier in this chapter the sig-

nificance of presuppositions in our interpretational endeavor and the importance of being able to identify them. This is not always easy to do when we confine our dialogue largely to those who agree with us, who may share the same presuppositions we do. They do not see our presuppositions any more than we do. To them as to us, these are not presuppositions, but simply aspects of the way things are, or in this case, the way the text is. The danger of unconscious eisegesis becomes even greater, for we are unaware of the starting points of our exegetical effort, which color the very way we see the text.

Cross-cultural dialogue can make us aware of some of these presuppositions, simply by virtue of the other person not seeing what we see in the text. That failure to see may, of course, simply be a result of the sort of cultural blindness that we spoke about above. It may, on the other hand, be because what we find there is not in the text, but is imported by us to the endeavor. Indeed, in that case our partner in the discussion will not see it there.

One Japanese pastor, who is quite a scholar and teaches regularly at a theological seminary, has often engaged in dialogue with an American seminary professor of his Baptist denomination. On one occasion, the two men were discussing Baptist distinctives and polity. The Japanese man told his American friend, "Your view of priesthood of the believer is derived more from the American Bill of Rights than it is from the New Testament." It is not my intention here to attempt to evaluate the two positions. The point is that the Japanese man may be right, but he also may be guilty of reading Japanese political conceptions into the New Testament. The value of this dialogue is that it points out the importance of cultural presuppositions and cross-cultural conversations.

3. Part of the reason for the increased insight resulting from cross-cultural dialogue is that those from other backgrounds frequently are asking different questions than we are. Part of what enables us to discover the meaning of the passage is the questions that we pose of the passage. We must be careful not to force the passage to answer questions that were not part of the original statement, either directly or by implication. Yet having said that, there is a richness to the passage that may be lost if we

fail to ask the various possible questions that could be addressed to it, to see all of what it does say.

This is where cross-cultural dialogue can be of particular help to us, for given a different background there will be different concerns and questions. The larger the number of perspectives from which the text is approached, the greater the possibility that we will avoid overlooking any one of them. We have seen of late, for example, that third world and especially Latin American liberation theologians have addressed questions regarding the equity of use and distribution of resources to the text and found that God has considerably more to say about such matters than some Europeans and North Americans had thought to be the case. This was simply because, not feeling the urgency of the issue, they had read right past or through the text and had not seen its meaning.

5

A New Paradigm?

Postmodernism and Hermeneutics

Different times and different contexts call for differing approaches to hermeneutics. Part of this is a result of the fact that the issues change. The propositions and values that are challenged today become the ones that must be defended, modified, or abandoned tomorrow. With the change of ideologies in the twentieth century, differing issues have risen to the fore.

At first these shifting issues were within a basically fixed framework. To a large extent, they were within the area of agreement between premodern and modern views of things. Now, however, it appears that we may be seeing not simply a shift in the orientation of thought, but an actual alteration of the framework within which thought takes place—a paradigm shift, as it were.[1] If this is the case, then the issues of hermeneutics must be investigated and pursued on a much broader scale than previously.

---

1. Nancey Murphy and James Wm. McClendon, Jr., "Distinguishing Modern and Postmodern Theologies," *Modern Theology* 5/3 (April 1989): 191.

99

The Premodern and Modern Periods

The premodern and modern periods basically agreed on a number of issues. They agreed, for example, on the objectivity of reality. Despite differences regarding the basis and status of this reality, there was at least agreement that such a reality existed independently of any individual apprehension of it. There also was a referential understanding of language, the belief that language referred to something beyond itself, that it had an object. Finally, wrapped up with these two tenets or assumptions was belief in a correspondence theory of truth, that is, the view that true ideas are those that accurately correspond to the state of affairs as it is.[2]

There were, of course, some very significant points of difference. For example, the locus of this truth or meaning was thought of very differently in the two periods under consideration. The premodern period fixed this objective meaning in some external or transcendent realm. This might be the Platonic forms or ideas, or in more theistic and even Christian versions, the mind of God. In either case, however, there was such a locus of meaning and truth outside history and the flow of nature's occurrences. If the premodern version was basically Platonic in its orientation, the modern period was more nearly Aristotelian. The rationalist approach, most clearly and consistently represented by Descartes, found the universal or objective factors of meaning in a pattern of reason or thought, in which the order of the human mind corresponded to that of reality. In empiricism, most fully enunciated by Hume, the aim was to find constant patterns of experience in the world, from which the laws of nature might then be derived. Finally, the humanists have taken a wide variety of positions, from Schleiermacher to Kierkegaard, but all of them located this objective or

2. Edgar V. McKnight, *Post-modern Use of the Bible: The Emergence of Reader-Oriented Criticism* (Nashville: Abingdon, 1988), pp. 43–44; Murphy and McClendon, "Distinguishing Modern and Postmodern Theologies," pp. 192–93; David Ray Griffin, "Postmodern Theology and A/Theology: A Response to Mark C. Taylor," in *Varieties of Postmodern Theology* by David Ray Griffin, William A. Beardslee, and Joe Holland (Albany: State University of New York Press, 1989), pp. 32–34; Mark C. Taylor, *Erring: A Postmodern A/theology* (Chicago: University of Chicago Press, 1984), pp. 172–80.

universal meaning in the self or the individual, in certain psychological characteristics common to all human beings. If the premodern view looked for the universals in a realm transcendent to nature and sensory experience, the modern view sought it within this experienced realm.[3]

Correlated with these conceptions were certain agreements and disagreements hermeneutically. In the premodern period, the meaning of a text was believed to be within that text in a rather literal or straightforward fashion. Thus, the meaning of the text was that which the author intended, and which a literal (or at least natural) rendering of the meaning of the words would yield. Hermeneutics was in this approach virtually equivalent to exegesis. If we could determine what the author had said, that was the message of the passage to us as well. While this is something of an oversimplification, it is basically the way meaning was understood and approached.

Modernism, however, developed more sophisticated—or at least more complicated—approaches to hermeneutics. Specifically, the prime methodology of modernism was historical criticism in all its variations and refinements. Historical criticism sought to determine the real history, what had really happened and what had really been said.[4] The true meaning of the text was not necessarily its surface or apparent meaning, but what the text said when properly interpreted and evaluated. Yet here there was at least agreement with the premodern conception that the goal of interpretation is to get at the truth and the meaning that was objective and resident in the text or behind it, rather than in the interpreter.[5]

Defining Postmodernism

Postmodernism has many different meanings; or, more correctly, a variety of views lay claim to the title of postmodernism. What all of them have in common is an agreement that modernism, however that is understood, has run its course. That is to

3. William Dean, *History Making History: The New Historicism in American Religious Thought* (Albany: State University of New York Press, 1988), p. 4.
4. McKnight, *Post-modern Use of the Bible,* p. 44.
5. Ibid.

say, intellectual work, whether that be literature, architecture, or theology, can no longer be carried on within the context of the modern worldview.[6]

This postmodernism has been identified as a number of sub-movements or concurrent and parallel movements in various disciplines. One of these is the school of literary criticism known as deconstruction. This can be seen as a reaction to structuralism, especially identified with the writings of Jacques Derridá. A second is a movement in the discipline of history known as the new historicism, associated especially with the work of Richard Rorty. A third is the philosophical movement known as neopragmatism, which includes such diverse cultural developments as the architecture of Michael Graves and Stanley Tigerman and the films of David Lynch.

There are a number of postmodern theologies. These can be classified, to some extent, by the degree of radicalness of their understanding of the change needed from the modern period. Thus, they range from deconstructive postmodernism to resto-rationist or conservative postmodernism. The classification given by David Ray Griffin is helpful here.[7]

1. Deconstructive postmodernism maintains that an attempt to take an objective approach to the facts of experience leads to the paradoxical conclusion that such an objective approach is not possible. It represents a radical denial of the objectivity in-volved in foundationalism, according to which there are certain basic or foundational facts to which thought can appeal, and the aim of thought is to base reasoning on such foundational truths. In this view language does not refer to objective objects as its ref-erents; words refer only to other words. In literary criticism and in theology, therefore, the aim is to "deconstruct" the traditional objects of thought and the traditional methods of the discipline. The usual criteria of internal consistency and coherence are not highly valued; in fact, they are believed to be inapplicable. In-stead, meaning is sought in the free associations of words.

6. Gary L. Comstock, "Is Postmodern Religious Dialogue Possible?" *Faith and Philosophy* 6/2 (April 1989): 196, n. 1.
7. David Ray Griffin, "Introduction: Varieties of Postmodern Theology," in *Varieties of Postmodern Theology* (Albany: State University of New York Press, 1989), pp. 1–7.

2. Liberationist postmodernism focuses more on the social and political form of the modern worldview, than the philosophical or metaphysical form. It reacts against these social structures, and seeks to transform them. Whether third world, black, or feminist in basic orientation, this postmodernism rejects the mind-set of the modern period. Although it does not reject the search for logical consistency and objective truth quite so emphatically as does deconstructive postmodernism, liberationist postmodernism does not value such qualities as highly as does modernism.

3. Constructive postmodernism seeks to rebuild or revise the modern worldview. It does not believe that such metaphysics is valid and defensible, but maintains that the construction of a worldview is possible. The form this constructive approach takes is frequently that of process metaphysics.

4. There is finally a version of postmodernism that can be referred to as conservative or restorationist. This postmodern theology, like constructive postmodernism, insists that much within the modern synthesis is worth retaining. It contends, however, that those elements most worth keeping are those that have most in common with the premodern period. It therefore seeks to reconstruct theology by going beyond modernism, building on those elements while transcending others. It appears on the surface to be a return to the premodern period, but that is not really true. This view maintains that the modern worldview reflects certain basic changes in the world that cannot be ignored or disregarded. They represent appropriate and irreversible changes in our way of thinking about reality. However, at points, the course of development of these correct insights is regarded as faulty.

The Importance of Postmodernism to Evangelicalism

It would seem that the most serious threat to orthodox or evangelical Christianity comes from deconstructive postmodernism. Yet because it is so radical, some believe that it really poses no threat to evangelical Christianity. We must ask, however, whether this is really so. A number of indications suggest that this is a very vital issue for evangelicalism.

First, the magnitude of the issues is so great. What is at stake is the very foundation of knowledge, at least as we have understood it, and probably universally in terms of objective, communicable truth. We are not talking merely about a different way of playing the game, but about altering the very rules of the game, about changing the actual game. The essence of the gospel includes certain rational beliefs and the ability to communicate them so that others may believe. If deconstruction succeeds, the gospel will deteriorate into a virtual solipsism. In a sense, the very future of Western culture may depend on the outcome of this struggle.[8]

Second, the effect of deconstructive postmodernism is more widespread than we may realize. We are accustomed to appealing to people on the basis of logical consistency and inconsistency. In certain varieties of thought, however, and especially in deconstruction, logical consistency is not seen as a virtue or inconsistency as a vice. This phenomenon is present on a rather broad basis within our society, however. The baby bust generation is not at all fazed by being confronted with the fact of logical inconsistency.[9]

Third, there is a tendency for evangelicalism to assimilate trends that at first are seen as antithetical to its basic view. This is what Roger Lundin has called "evangelical culture-lag." He points out that what evangelicals condemn when it first appears, they eventually come to adopt, with some variations, whether it be television, music, or philosophy.[10] He raises the possibility that, based on the past pattern of response, "in only a few years we may be hearing the sanctified deconstructive word from Christian critics."[11] The earlier tendency toward antithesis and rejection has in more recent years given way to

8. John N. Wall, "Deconstruction and the Universe of Theological Discourse, or, Who Is Jacques Derrida and What Is He Saying about the Logos?" *The St. Luke's Journal of Theology* 28/4 (Sept. 1985): 253–54.

9. Leith Anderson, *Dying for Change* (Minneapolis: Bethany House, 1990), pp. 107–8.

10. Roger Lundin, "Deconstructive Therapy," *The Reformed Journal* 36/1 (Jan. 1986): 15–16. See, for example, the criticism of television by Edward John Carnell, *Television: Servant or Master* (Grand Rapids: Eerdmans, 1950), a book he never later listed with his works, and *The Case for Orthodox Theology* (Philadelphia: Westminster, 1959), p. 121.

11. Ibid., p. 16.

adoption and absorption, and this might even be true of something as radical as deconstructionism.

The Erosion of the Modern Synthesis

At this point we need to examine more closely the nature of the modernism now being rejected and displaced. It was a major synthesis, resulting from scientific, philosophical, and political developments.

1. The first major emphasis of modernism was the centrality and autonomy of the human. In the premodern period, theology, especially of the Calvinistic variety, had emphasized the centrality of God and his sovereignty or free and absolute will. Modernism shifted attention to the human. Here was the center of attention and thought. Here was the highest value. Here was the one in control of what went on within the universe. Neither the church's authority nor God's commands could be allowed to encroach on this human.[12]

2. Together with this emphasis on the human was a great interest in nature, the appropriate habitat and natural setting for the human.[13] As the focus of attention shifted from God to humans, so the center of activity shifted from the heavenly or ethereal realm to the earthly. With the abandonment of asceticism came a great interest in the earth and nature. The drama of life was to be acted out on this stage.

3. With this growing interest in nature, a method for investigating it also had to be developed. Thus the scientific method became the major means of gaining knowledge.[14] While some saw this as only one way of knowing, for others it became the paradigm or virtually the only method for investigating truth. This is seen in the effort by disciplines other than the natural sciences to adopt this same methodology. Behavioral sciences, for example, came to use the experimental procedure when possible, and sought to employ statistical methods to reduce findings to a mathematically quantifiable form.

---

12. John Herman Randall, Jr., *The Making of the Modern Mind* (Boston: Houghton Mifflin, 1940), pp. 123–24.
13. Ibid., pp. 226–27.
14. Ibid., pp. 219–24.

Where science was seen as only one of the appropriate ways of knowing, it was frequently seen as superior to others, the methods of philosophy and other inquiries being "soft" in nature. In some views, however, science was thought to be the only legitimate means of knowledge. Whatever did not measure up to its standards and come through its channels was not really knowledge at all.

4. Together with these concepts and binding them together was the idea of nature as dynamic, and as the sole and sufficient cause and explanation of what is and what transpires. The concept of evolution was used to explain human origins. Rather than being the product of some special supernatural act of creation, the human was understood to have evolved from other living forms, to be a part of nature bound by natural laws.[15]

5. A growing conception was that of determinism or the absolute causation within the whole of the universe. As science studied this universe, it increasingly discovered fixed and regular patterns within it. This led to the assumption of uniformity or regularity or complete causation in nature. Research that proceeded on this assumption proved fruitful in its results. The assumption was that the patterns observed in the parts of reality that could be thus investigated also extended to those parts that could not be similarly observed, or had not yet been investigated.[16]

6. There also was a tendency toward reductionism, the effort to explain everything by fewer or more basic factors. Thus, psychology has tended to reduce to biology, biology to chemistry, chemistry to physics.[17]

7. There also was, in common with the earlier understanding, a belief in foundationalism. This is the idea that knowledge must be justified by being based on certain indubitable or incorrigible beliefs. The task of the philosopher has often been seen as a search for such indubitability. For Descartes, the foundations of knowledge were seen as intuitions of clear and distinct ideas. For Hume, on the other hand, the source of knowledge

15. Ibid., pp. 465–66.
16. Ibid.
17. Murphy and McClendon, "Distinguishing Modern and Postmodern Theologies," pp. 197–98.

was sense impressions. While Hume seemed, when compared to rationalists such as Descartes, to be something of a skeptic, he too was searching for and believed he had found, a sound basis for belief. The logical positivists, in their early days, were seeking for such a certainty in sense data.[18]

8. There was basically a belief in metaphysical realism. Physical objects were believed to have a real existence apart from our perception of them. They are there to be known, simply because they are. These objects, which are apprehended by us through sense perception, are therefore real.[19]

9. There was the representative-expressivist theory of language. Language, on this way of thinking, has as its primary role representing that to which it refers. Language names objects and represents facts about these objects. There are, however, some areas, such as ethics, where, although the grammatical form of the sentences may seem to indicate representation, that is not an adequate way of understanding the role of language. Here the role of language is actually to express the feeling or emotion of the speaker. Hence, the reference is not to the ostensive referent, but to inward states or intentions of the speaker.[20]

10. Finally, the modern view presupposed a correspondence theory of truth. That is to say, those propositions are true that correctly reflect or correspond to things as they really are.[21] To be sure, this was at times supplemented and even competed with by the pragmatic theory of truth, but even William James' first definition of truth in his essay on pragmatism is essentially a correspondence view: "Truth, as any dictionary will tell you, is a property of certain of our ideas. It means their 'agreement,' as falsity means their disagreement, with 'reality.'"[22] This suggests that the pragmatist view of truth was more a theory about testing for truth than an attempt to delineate the nature of truth.

This modern worldview has gradually begun to erode. Slowly at first, and then with accelerating pace of late, the inadequacies of this understanding of reality have been revealed.

18. Ibid., pp. 192–93.
19. Dean, *History Making History*, pp. 6–7.
20. Ibid., pp. 192–96.
21. Timothy Reiss, *The Discourse of Modernism* (Ithaca, N.Y.: Cornell University Press, 1985), p. 44.
22. William James, *Pragmatism* (New York: Meridian, 1955), p. 132.

The acceptance of the idea that the modern period is passing away has become increasingly widespread. The significance of this change should not be overlooked or minimized. We are not witnessing merely the displacement of one theory by another, or a conflict about some peripheral ideas. We are actually seeing a paradigm shift taking place before our eyes. The conceptions on the basis of which society has functioned for some time are changing. As Diogenes Allen puts it, "What is crumbling are the pillars of western society, which were erected during the Enlightenment."[23] We need to observe first the reasons for this collapse, so that we may understand what is happening and why, and then look at which conceptions may survive, which conceptions may need to be adapted, and which conceptions will surely pass away completely.

It appears that there have been both theoretical or rational and practical or moral reasons for this disillusionment with modernism. The four areas of breakdown mentioned by Allen are helpful here as an organizing basis for our thought.[24]

First, the idea of the universe as a self-contained entity has broken down. The modern view included the idea that all of reality functioned according to certain fixed patterns. These natural laws were even thought of in some cases as controlling what happened. A number of factors have combined to undercut this conception, however.

One of these was Heisenberg's principle of indeterminacy. At the subatomic level, the behavior of particles or electrical charges appears unpredictable. Random factors seem to be present at this level. In addition, the Big Bang theory suggests that the entire universe was at one time very dense, concentrated in one place.[25]

Second, the modern approach appears to have failed morally. A number of social problems remain unsolved, and if anything, are becoming progressively worse and more threatening.

23. Diogenes Allen, "Christian Values in a Post-Christian Context," in *Postmodern Theology: Christian Faith in a Pluralist World* (San Francisco: Harper and Row, 1989), p. 21.

24. Ibid., pp. 21–25.

25. David Ray Griffin, *God and Religion in the Postmodern World: Essays in Postmodern Theology* (Albany: State University of New York Press, 1989), p. 36.

War, which once was a local matter with relatively few casualties, has now become literally a global concern. The war to end all wars, the Great World War, turned out to be World War I; it was succeeded by an even more expansive conflict, World War II. Improved means of communication and transportation made possible wider geographical involvement and modern means of destruction made possible more efficient killing of humans and devastation of property. It was not necessarily that persons were morally worse than before, but they now had more effective weapons available. Human ingenuity seemed most productive when geared to making war.

It also became apparent that we have been destroying our home, the very environment in which we dwell. The accelerated consumption of nonrenewable resources and the poisoning of the environment suggested that this world may not be able to sustain human life indefinitely.[26]

The potential of nuclear destruction hangs like a spectre over the human race. Although the apparent end of the cold war has greatly reduced the possibility of a nuclear confrontation between superpowers, the danger of the spread of nuclear capability to terrorist groups is in some ways even more ominous.

In the midst of this, the failure to solve society's economic problems is ever apparent. The progress and prosperity of society as a whole do not extend to the poor, who are relegated to a structural underclass.

In all of this the problem is not simply the failure to solve specific problems, but the inability of modern thought to provide an adequate basis for morality. The decline in transcendent norms and the emphasis upon individualism have not facilitated the sort of consensus necessary for moral action in a pluralistic society. In part, the tendency toward mechanism in the worldview has been a factor in this difficulty.

Third, there has been a loss of belief in virtually inevitable progress. Inspired by the industrial revolution and supported in part by the extension of Darwinism to cover the development of all facets of culture, there was an expectation that things would get better and better and that social problems would wither

26. Joe Holland, "The Postmodern Paradigm and Contemporary Catholicism," in *Varieties of Postmodern Theology,* pp. 11–12.

away. This, however, simply has not happened. For the first time a new generation has discovered that its standard of living will be lower than that of the preceding generation; disillusionment with the "great American dream" has begun to set in.

Fourth, the assumption that knowledge is inherently good has also come to be questioned. It is apparent that knowledge can be used for good or evil, and that an increase in knowledge will not automatically result in a better world. Even on a microscale, the standard assumption that a college education will lead to a better job and more money is proving uncertain. The increase in overall knowledge has helped somewhat, but to some extent has simply heightened the discrepancies between various social classes.

The most radical rejection of this modern view—and consequently, the most strongly contrasting alternative—is what we have identified as deconstructive or eliminative postmodernism. It draws its inspiration from a number of sources. This type of postmodern theology and biblical hermeneutic is described by its leading practitioner, Mark Taylor, as the hermeneutic of the death of God.[27] It takes seriously the avowedly atheistic philosophy of Derridá. It then attempts to spell out the implications of God's death. Taylor says, "The insights released by deconstructive criticism suggest the ramifications of the death of God for areas as apparently distinct as contemporary psychology, linguistics, historical analysis."[28]

The Hermeneutic of Deconstruction

It will not be my purpose to spell out the implications of deconstruction for all areas of thought, or even for all doctrines. I do want to note its view of language and hence of hermeneutics. There is no longer one unifying center or basis of meaning. Thus, there is no basis for distinguishing one perspective as superior to another. Consequently, there is no truth. This does not mean merely that we cannot know the truth, but rather that there is no truth to know. There is no linguistic Archimedean point "to provide access to a nonfigural world that can function

27. Mark C. Taylor, *Erring* (Chicago: University of Chicago Press, 1984), p. 6.
28. Ibid.

as the critical norm with which to judge conflicting configurations."[29] There is no such thing as raw experience. There are only interpretations of interpretations. There is nothing absolutely primary to be interpreted.[30]

Richard Rorty notes that the ancient cosmologists held that the world rested on the back of an elephant. One of them, when asked what the elephant rested on, replied, "It's elephants all the way down." This, says Rorty, is how it is with language. There is no basic or ultimate reality upon which words rest. Rather, "It's words all the way down." Words do not rest upon anything more basic. Their referent is more words.[31]

This is Taylor's view. Without the "transcendental signified," there is nothing that grounds the structure of signification.[32] Not merely the deduction from the death of God, but also an analysis of the nature of experience itself leads us to the conclusion of the nonreferential nature of language. It shows us that there is no such thing as raw experience or naked facts. Every sign is already an interpretation of other interpretations.[33]

Consciousness, it becomes apparent, is creative and productive. It does not find meaning or criteria external to itself, but, rather, within itself. "That to which consciousness points is always already within consciousness itself."[34] Thus, instead of attempting to arrive at the inherent meaning of a text, perhaps placed there intentionally by the author, the interpreter engages in a free play of consciousness.[35]

Hermeneutics, then, consists in word-play and word-associations. Taylor especially likes to trace the etymology of a word, or to list all of its possible meanings. He plays with words, utilizing puns, hyphens, slashes, and parentheses to draw out possible meanings. Since there is no correspondence theory of truth, no objects to which the words refer, the consciousness of the interpreter creates the meanings out of itself. Like his literary mentor,

29. Ibid., p. 172.

30. Ibid.

31. Richard Rorty, *Consequences of Nature: Essays 1972–1980* (Minneapolis: University of Minnesota Press, 1982), p. xxxv.

32. Ibid., p. 105.

33. Ibid., p. 172.

34. Ibid., p. 105.

35. Ibid., p. 106.

Derridá, Taylor holds that the use of language is generative of meaning. He gives an initial example of his method by taking the word "err" and roaming "through the labyrinth of the word," seeking thereby to gain an understanding of its meaning.[36]

It should be apparent that this view is incompatible with the orthodox or conservative understanding not only of Scripture and hermeneutics, but consequently of all hermeneutical tenets. If Taylor's view is followed, then there really cannot be any objective truth, any objects of knowledge, anything that applies to everyone.

Critical Evaluation of Deconstructive Postmodernism

In response, there need to be two coincident but distinguishable parts of the hermeneutical task. Because the deconstructive version of postmodernism is the most radical, calling into question most completely the theological and specifically the hermeneutical endeavor, there will need to be a careful evaluation and refutation of that movement. Second, there will need to be constructive work to formulate an alternative—a genuinely postmodern evangelical hermeneutic. In this latter endeavor, we will find that there are some very disturbing elements in the present environment, as well as some that present us with unprecedented opportunity.

We begin with a critical evaluation of deconstructive postmodernism. Here we immediately face an especially difficult consideration. The problem is this: the very grounds of criticism and evaluation seem to presuppose the objective factors being challenged by this movement. Presumably, therefore, we would not be able to engage in dialogue with these deconstructionists. We would only be able to maintain our own separate and different positions.[37]

There may yet be a basis for evaluation, however. It is not fair to criticize a view simply because it does not meet the criteria of our view. It is, however, legitimate to criticize a view if

36. Ibid., pp. 11–13.
37. Wall, "Deconstruction and the Universe of Theological Discourse," pp. 253–54.

it contradicts some more universal criteria, criteria that all views must satisfy. It is also legitimate to criticize a view on the basis of its own criteria—an application of the law of contradiction, which itself is necessary if any communication is to take place, or, I would suggest, if any thought is even to proceed. The postmodernists have engaged us in conversation, seeking to present their view as an alternative to the traditional (premodern or modern) view. They are not simply solipsists. We are therefore justified in inquiring about the elements presupposed and present within such communication. In other words, we may begin with practical problems inherent in thinking and communicating, and move from these to the more theoretical issues.

One person who has presented a criticism of deconstruction from another postmodern perspective is David Ray Griffin. He argues that there are certain facts, which are acknowledged in practice, even if denied verbally. They are universally acknowledged in what he calls hard-core commonsense notions. They are commonsense because they are common to all humanity. They are to be distinguished from soft-core commonsense notions, which are not actually universal but are in fact provincial, and can be denied without inconsistency. The latter include ideas such as that the sun goes around the earth, the species are eternal, and rocks have no feelings. They are not held by all persons, and can be denied without contradiction. A truly hard-core commonsense notion, on the other hand, cannot be denied without contradicting one's practice. Griffin suggests four hard-core commonsense notions:

> Included among the hard-core notions common to every person, I claim, are the following: (1) that the person has *freedom*, in the sense of some power for self-determination; (2) that there is an *actual world* beyond the person's present experience which exists independently of and exerts causal efficacy upon that person's interpretive perception of it; (3) that one's interpretive ideas are *true* to the degree that they correspond to that independently existing world; and (4) that, for at least some events, a distinction exists between what happened and *better and/or worse* things that could have happened. If it is true that these notions are presupposed in practice by everyone, we would ex-

pect Taylor's denial of them to be accompanied by statements in which they are implicitly affirmed.[38]

We may wish to take issue with the specific notions Griffin proposes, or the way he implements his criticism. In particular, I would include certain laws of logic, which are implicitly assumed in Griffin's utilization of the idea of inconsistency as a criterion. It does appear to me, however, that this is a direction in which we will need to go.

It is here that we can enlist the services of persons who are primarily philosophers rather than hermeneuts. We may want to look to the Society of Christian Philosophers for help in these matters, as they will be concerned increasingly with the type of issues raised by deconstructive postmodernism.[39]

Guidelines for a Postmodern Evangelical Hermeneutic

The second part of our task will be to develop guidelines for a postmodern hermeneutic. This hermeneutic will resemble premodern hermeneutics at a number of points but will be a genuinely postmodern approach in terms of working from within postmodernism, taking seriously its contentions and either developing responses to the valid points within them, taking them to their logical conclusions and showing their untenability, or simply attempting to rebut them. It will need to be an approach that takes seriously the changes that have taken place in our world, not only in the last four centuries, but also in the last four decades. I am not here developing a full-fledged hermeneutic, but rather merely seeking to outline some guidelines or principles that will need to be embodied in a postmodern hermeneutic, and to offer some preliminary suggestions for implementing them. This will be really more a plea than a product.

1. First, the rejection of foundationalism must be taken seriously. Foundationalism assumes that there are some absolute or

38. Griffin, "Introduction: Varieties of Postmodern Theology," p. 36.
39. See, for example, the classic criticism of subjectivism presented by Donald Davidson, "On the Very Idea of a Conceptual System," *Proceedings and Addresses of the American Philosophical Association* 47 (Nov. 1974): 5–20.

nonrelative tenets upon which knowledge can be based. These tenets do not require any assumptions being made, but rather are indubitable first truths, or something similar.

Recent thought has challenged this concept.[40] It now appears that some of the things considered so indubitable are actually assumptions, and the conclusions drawn relative to those assumptions. Einstein, for example, formulated his theory of relativity out of the paradox of addition of velocities. Velocities should be cumulative, so that the speed of closure of light from a star moving toward the observer should be greater than that of the light from a star revolving away. Yet this proved not to be the case. Einstein proposed that we reject the underlying assumptions of the absoluteness of time and space. Instead, he suggested that time and space are relative. This set of assumptions was validated by more nearly fitting the empirical data, than by some sort of absolute justification.[41]

Careful analysis of language, for example, reveals that differences of opinion on a subject are frequently based on differing definitions of terms, and differing conceptions injected into the argument as premises that often are hidden, both from the speaker and the listener. Even William James pointed out that the two men arguing about whether the squirrel went around the man were not differing about a matter of fact, but about the interpretation thereof.[42] The large number of persons who argue for differing conclusions using the same set of data also underscore this point.

The number of truly foundational items will have to be considerably reduced. Rather than being substantive in nature, these may turn out to be more methodological. They may be logical or linguistic assumptions that we cannot deny without assuming them in the process, or without resorting to sheer authoritarianism or dogmatism.

Our approach may need to be more like that of presuppositionalism than of traditional foundationalism. We may need to

40. Richard Rorty, "A Reply to Dreyfus and Taylor," *The Review of Metaphysics* 34 (1980): 39.

41. James B. Miller, "The Emerging Postmodern World," in *Postmodern Theology: Christian Faith in a Pluralist World*, ed. Frederic C. Burnham (San Francisco: Harper and Row, 1989), p. 9.

42. James, *Pragmatism*, pp. 41–42.

assume a tenet or a system of such tenets, trace out the implications of such assumptions, and show how these assumptions and the systems that derive from them are more consistent and coherent and fit the broad sweep of experience more adequately than do competitive views. The exhibition of the truth of a position will be less likely a deductive demonstration from first principles, than an inductive fit of the facts.

2. This hermeneutic will examine closely what language signs signify. The modern view has been that they correspond to objects—not necessarily physical objects, but objects inhering within the natural world of experience. The postmodern view has tended to identify the objects of words as other words, rather than nonverbal referents. It may be that the time has come to challenge both conceptions.

I would suggest that what we think of as the referent of our language is the concept. Rather than referring to an actual chair, the word "chair" refers to the concept of a chair, or chairness. While a given chair may take into account several subconcepts (such as metal material, brown color, etc.), these subconcepts only serve to refine the idea of chair.

In actuality, this parallels the way languages are taught to nonspeakers. These nonspeakers may represent many different native languages, so no one language is common to all of them. The instructor points to an object and gives the English word for the object (assuming that English is the language being taught and learned). Thus, the German-speaking student does not think "*das Fenster* = the window." He merely looks at the object and thinks, "the window." Or, conversely, he now hears the word "window," and does not think "*das Fenster*," but, rather, visualizes the object.

On the surface of it, this may seem to be an uncritical or precritical return to an ancient Platonism. There is a strong parallel to that or some other Greek philosophies, but what is emerging here is a contemporary form based on recent insights but preserving that which was true and correct and insightful from that ancient philosophy.

Let us now look at the implications of this insight for hermeneutics. What we most certainly are not denying is the concept of verbal inspiration in favor of some sort of dynamic or conceptual view. The very words of Scripture are those intended by God to be written by the writer in order to convey the message He wished. The real locus of that revelation, however, is the ideas or concepts that the written words convey. This suggests that we have not finished the hermeneutical or even the exegetical task when we have explained the passage in its original setting. We must ask about the underlying concept. Thus, for example, the meaning of Genesis 22 is not merely that God commanded Abraham to offer his son, and that he provided a sacrifice as a substitute. That is certainly being taught, and the historical fact ought not to be denied or minimized. However, Genesis 22 also teaches us about the holiness of God, his expectation of obedience from his followers, and his faithfulness.

This will already take us a major portion of the way toward making the biblical teaching applicable to other times and places. This has the potential for making the message truly cross-cultural. What is translated into these different settings is less like a given language and more like what is translated from one language to another.

One contemporary source for this insight is the success of the case study method of teaching. By looking at case studies we are forced to inquire about more general principles, which can then be transferred. We will need to interpret the narrative portions and the didactic portions written to specific situations as case studies. The application portion of our hermeneutic will proceed using the same techniques utilized in the study of cases.

3. A postmodern hermeneutic will also need to take into account the fact that meaningfulness (as contrasted with meaning) or significance (as contrasted with signification) is the main issue today for many people. For such people, the primary question is not, "Is it true?" but rather, "Does it matter?"[43] Whether this ought to be the primary question is not the issue. The point is that hermeneutics must address the question of the relevance of a given truth to individuals and groups. There is plenty of

---

43. Joe Holland, "The Postmodern Paradigm and Contemporary Catholicism," in *Varieties of Postmodern Theology*, by David Ray Griffin, William A. Beardslee, and Joe Holland (Albany: State University of New York Press, 1989), pp. 11–12.

room for demonstrating that apart from the question of truthfulness, relevance is immaterial.

It should be observed in this connection that the question of meaningfulness versus meaning and of significance versus signification is not a question of time. Perhaps through the concepts propounded by Hirsch we have tended to equate meaning and significance with meaning then and meaning now, but such really should not be the case.[44] There is both past meaning and meaningfulness, and present meaning and meaningfulness. It is a matter of showing the implications of propositions for our lives.

4. It may well be that the meaning of biblical propositions will not always be in terms of showing the meaning of each individual statement. Rather, it may be a matter of showing the meaning and meaningfulness of the scheme as a whole, and then showing the relationship of individual parts to that whole.

This insight comes from two sources. It has often been thought that the meaning of language was to be found in the meaning of the individual units or words. Logical positivism modified this by contending that the proposition, rather than the word, was the basic unit of meaning. Now, however, it is apparent, based on some of the insights of narrative literary interpretation, that the unit must be made even broader, extended to the whole story. Without that, details may seem insignificant. The pertinence of the story as a whole can be shown in ways in which individual segments of it cannot.

The other source from which this insight is drawn is the theology of Wolfhart Pannenberg. Pannenberg has developed a concept of revelation in which the whole of history is revelatory, not merely certain elements or motifs within it. Yet the meaning of history is seen at the end, not at the beginning or some intermediate point.[45] Without necessarily espousing Pannenberg's view of revelation and history, it is possible to see

44. E. D. Hirsch, Jr., *Validity in Interpretation* (New Haven: Yale University Press, 1967), p. 8.

45. Wolfhart Pannenberg, "Dogmatic Theses on the Doctrine of Revelation," in *Revelation as History*, ed. Wolfhart Pannenberg (New York: Macmillan, 1968), pp. 131–35.

that the meaning of any story depends on the outcome, and the content of a message requires the conclusion.

5. The significance or meaningfulness of biblical texts will be demonstrated by showing their relationship to fundamental human needs.

What are these fundamental human needs? These needs are such things as the need to feel we have significance as individuals. In a day in which corporations and governmental agencies tend to treat persons as simply members of groups or masses of people, the biblical emphasis on the God who knows the very number of the hairs of our heads (Matt. 10:30), who knows when one bird falls to the earth (Matt. 10:29), who knows his sheep and calls them by name (John 10:3) is an important response to this deep human longing. The need for forgiveness, not just for individual acts against individual persons but for cosmic forgiveness, is responded to by the teaching, "though your sins be as scarlet, they shall be as white as snow." The sense that we are just ordinary, not excelling in anything and therefore unimportant and unloved, is responded to by the teaching that God made each of us in his own image, using himself as the pattern for our creation; God gave his own Son, who died for us and in our place. Such teaching confers dignity. Our sense that our lives have no value, since everything we have done during them will simply perish when we die, is responded to by the doctrine of the second coming, the resurrection, and the eternal future state. It is important that these points of meaningfulness be established at least as a starting point for our explanation and presentation of the meaning of the biblical message.

In some cases this may be done with specific texts. In other cases, it may be accomplished by showing how the system as a whole serves this role. The remainder of the texts will have their meaningfulness by virtue of their coherent participation in the whole.

It should be noted that while some portions of Scripture cannot be directly seen to have meaningfulness, they contribute to and are presupposed by the whole, which ultimately gives the meaningfulness. We may therefore hold to the meaningfulness of these biblical passages on the basis of the "slope of the evidence," as it were. The situation here is not greatly different from the approach of moderate harmonists on the matter of the phenomena, as these bear upon the doctrine of biblical inerrancy. We believe in the one group on the basis of the other and the trend of the validation.

6. We will also need increasingly to employ phenomenology as a method for identifying those dimensions of human experience to which the biblical material can be related. It is here that our hermeneutic will be postmodern rather than merely premodern, for it is our aim to take the experience of the modern person, or perhaps we should term it, the secular person, and demonstrate the fundamental human needs that are presupposed by it, or perhaps, which show around its edges.

One example of what we are advocating here is Langdon Gilkey's *Naming the Whirlwind*. While this is ostensibly a treatment of the problem of religious language, it gives us much more than that. It is a careful phenomenological analysis of modern secular experience. In the constructive portion of the work, Gilkey explores what he calls "The Dimension of Ultimacy in Secular Experience." He shows that even within such secular experience there is that which transcends it, which goes beyond the limits of its own categories.[46] The modern secular person does not and cannot live entirely within the categories of his own system. There are elements of ultimacy that continue to appear around the fringes, as it were, of secular experience. There are four dimensions of this experience of ultimacy: the source or ground of what we are, the experience of our limits, the source and basis of our values, and the element of mystery. Gilkey cites such experiences as awe that we feel at the birth of a child, the awareness of our finiteness in the "midlife crisis," the awareness of possible nonbeing as we face death. All of these are elements of ultimacy. Such phenomenological analysis is appropriate in the postmodern period, and will be of assistance in showing the meaningfulness of the biblical revelation by relating it to such experiences as these.

7. One of the developments that science has recently produced is the breakdown of the conception of the universe as a

46. Langdon Gilkey, *Naming the Whirlwind: The Renewal of God-Language* (Indianapolis: Bobbs-Merrill, 1969), pp. 305–413.

self-sustaining, fixed, law-bound entity. The idea of absolute determinism has been affected by such factors as Heisenberg's principle of indeterminacy[47] and the "Big Bang."[48] Consequently, scientists have considerably adjusted their conception of natural laws. Rather than absolute, iron-clad, and invariable, these laws are now thought of more as statistical constants. They are inductive descriptions of how things ordinarily happen, rather than impenetrable determinants of how things must happen. In the former view, only natural explanations for any phenomenon could be accepted. Now, other possibilities cannot be excluded a priori.[49]

It is here that we must endeavor to be genuinely postmodern. Historical criticism was the supreme hermeneutical tool of the modern period. It sought to account for the production of a given portion of the text on the basis of what were basically natural factors. Thus, the laws that govern the formation and growth of oral tradition in various societies; the kinds of considerations that enter into an author's choice of one set of words or one form of expression in light of a particular audience; the influences of upbringing and culture—all of these are introduced as explanations for the particular content and reading of the text. The idea of a supernatural revelation of truth and of a supernatural guidance in the choice of wording does not really enter into the consideration of why the text says what it does.

While evangelicals have sometimes been quite categorical in their rejection of biblical criticism, many evangelical biblical scholars have in recent years adopted some of the methodology of the biblical critics. In so doing, however, they have usually emphasized their intention to practice great care not to adopt naturalistic or antisupernaturalistic assumptions. This has generally meant rejecting any antecedent objection to miracles. So the miracle narratives in the Bible have been taken seriously and the incidents considered to have potentially really occurred. Taking seriously belief in an omnipotent, transcendent

47. David Ray Griffin, *God and Religion in the Postmodern World: Essays in Postmodern Theology* (Albany: State University of New York Press, 1989), p. 36.
48. Allen, "Christian Values in a Post-Christian Context," p. 22.
49. Griffin, *God and Religion*, pp. 79–80.

God, this approach held that he was capable of doing anything, nature notwithstanding.

There is, however, a more subtle form in which naturalistic assumptions affect hermeneutics, even evangelical hermeneutics. That pertains to the explanation of the process of writing. It is quite possible to interpret the writing purely in terms of what natural factors would have led the writer to write what he did. In such a scheme, there would be no explanation of something that the writer could not have otherwise known on the grounds that God specially revealed that matter to the author. And, for that matter, there would not be an explanation of why one grammatical form was selected rather than another on the basis that the Holy Spirit guided the writer to make that selection. Sayings attributed to Jesus that do not appear in any known tradition available to the author may be interpreted as prophecies given by the resurrected and ascended Jesus to the author, rather than as specially revealed sayings that Jesus actually gave during his earthly ministry, but which do not occur in any of the traditions and of which the writer may not otherwise have been aware.[50] And discussions of authorial intent may treat the writing as if the human author is the sole author, without asking whether there may have been some additional, supernatural author.

It has not been easier in the past hundred years or so than it is now to accept the idea that God has supernaturally caused all that has occurred, including the production of the Bible.[51] It is important that any postmodern hermeneutic take seriously and seize the opportunities presented by modern developments in the understanding of causation within the universe.

8. A prized tenet of the modern era was the value of the individual.[52] The individual's freedom and initiative were not to be restricted in any sense. Hermeneutics was also often carried on

---

50. Gerald Hawthorne, "Christian Prophets and the Sayings of Jesus: Evidence of and Criteria for," *SBL Seminary Papers* (Missoula, Mont.: Scholars Press, 1975), 2:174–78.

51. Allen, "Christian Values in a Post-Christian Context," p. 22.

52. Joe Holland, "The Cultural Vision of Pope John Paul II: Toward a Conservative/Liberal Postmodern Dialogue," in *Varieties of Postmodern Theology*, p. 120; Murphy and McClendon, "Distinguishing Modern and Postmodern Theologies," pp. 196–98.

in an individualistic—and even ruggedly individualistic—fashion. Each person formulated his or her own interpretation of passages. These interpretations were, to be sure, submitted to colleagues for review and sometimes to peers in professional societies for critique, but it was still basically an individual effort, although informed by observations from others. This, it would seem, must change. Knowledge is exploding so rapidly that no one person can keep abreast of the developments. Also, all of us have limited perspectives. A model that comes to mind is the so-called Pannenberg circle of graduate students at Heidelberg in the early 1960s, which collaborated in the development of a doctrine of revelation. The same is possible with respect to hermeneutical treatments of passages of Scripture. Another illustration is the special interest groups within the American Academy of Religion and the Society of Biblical Literature. Scholars with similar interests gather together and work synergistically to produce understanding and scholarly publications on their area of interest.

9. There will also need to be a genuinely philosophical basis to the hermeneutical work that is done. It is essential that hermeneuts understand that genuinely ideational differences separate various hermeneutical systems. A given hermeneutic will need to be understood as part of a much larger system of thought, and that system will have to be carefully evaluated.

This means that postmodern hermeneuts will need to be more broadly prepared than in the past. Certainly the discipline of linguistics must inform what is done. Frequently, a given hermeneutic has not been adequately based on linguistic understanding. An example would be the Biblical Theology movement, and the devastating criticism leveled at it by James Barr.[53] It was drawing conclusions that rested on unsustainable conceptions of language. Today's and tomorrow's hermeneutics will require a better knowledge of linguistics.

Beyond that, however, more purely philosophical knowledge and endeavor will be necessary. A model for us, in some ways, will be the work done by Anthony Thiselton in his signif-

53. James Barr, *Semantics of Biblical Language* (New York: Oxford University Press, 1961).

icant books, *The Two Horizons* and *New Horizons in Hermeneutics.*[54] Thiselton displays an extensive understanding of the philosophical basis of several different hermeneutical approaches. Whether we agree with his conclusions or his purpose in engaging in this particular endeavor, we must certainly admire his philosophical sophistication. The type of hermeneutical work done in the future, whether of this same agenda or not, will certainly require the hermeneut to possess the resources and credentials that Thiselton displays in this work.

10. There will definitely need to be further development of what, for want of a better term, we might appropriately call "metahermeneutics." By this term is meant the discussion of hermeneutical theory, as opposed to the practice of hermeneutics. Much hermeneutics in the past has consisted of developing guidelines and rules for doing hermeneutics within a given framework or on a particular theoretical basis, and then of actually doing that interpretational work. What is really at stake in our present time, however, is the very framework, the very foundation, on which this endeavor rests. It is primarily here that the discussion and debate will have to move. Whether there can even be rules for interpretation, whether truth is primarily subjective or objective, where meaning resides, are the big issues that need treatment.

11. We will need to pay more attention to global or multicultural issues. While there is a danger that saying this could reflect merely a current fad, it is the case that in the postmodern period we are faced with large issues posed by greater contact with a divergence of cultures in our world.

In at least the initial stages of the modern period, an endeavor was made to find universal conceptions. The belief was, at least implicitly, that all humans thought the same way. Of course, not all humans had the same thoughts or agreed on every point, but the process of thinking, the way of looking at things, was the same.

54. Anthony Thiselton, *The Two Horizons: New Testament Hermeneutics and Philosophical Description with Special Reference to Heidegger, Bultmann, Gadamer, and Wittgenstein* (Grand Rapids: Eerdmans, 1980); *New Horizons in Hermeneutics* (Grand Rapids: Zondervan, 1992).

Our increased contact with a variety of cultures has shown us that there are actually different perceptions of reality. There is a different way of grasping, or integrating, or conceptualizing reality in such basic matters as space and time.[55] These preexperiential differences are also prereflective. When we interpret literature, such as a biblical passage, these differences affect at an unconscious level what we see and how we understand it. Anthropology, whether technical or popular (contact with other peoples), is making this increasingly clear.

What I have said need not lead to a relativistic or subjective understanding of truth. We are talking about one truth, but different people will look at that one truth from varying perspectives. They see some things, objectively there, which others do not. The results of these different perspectives are not contradictory, but complementary, insights.

This truth was brought home to me rather dramatically during a chapel series on the life of David. A woman New Testament scholar talked about David and Bathsheba. Taking the perspective of Bathsheba, she pointed out some facets of the biblical narrative that were in the text, but which I had never observed, simply because they were issues which, as a man, I did not think of. Anyone who has consulted several commentaries on a single passage of Scripture knows that different writers have very different insights. Not all of them comment on every dimension of the text, in many cases just because of limitations of space. Whether they see the other dimensions, or whether they choose not to develop them, is a function, however, of their own perspectives.

We have sometimes proceeded as if our interpretation of a given text is the way it is, the true and perhaps the only possible way to look at that text. In a postmodern world, a world in which Christianity is growing faster in the third world than it is in Europe and North America, we may discover that what we thought was the full meaning of the text was only the Western, white, middle-class, male, interpretation. A truly postmodern hermeneutic will need to be fully global and fully multicultural.

---

55. Ernst Cassirer, *An Essay on Man: An Introduction to a Philosophy of Human Culture* (Garden City, N.Y.: Doubleday, 1944), pp. 62–79.

Scripture Index

Genesis

1:28—70
9:6—58, 68
22—62, 64, 117
22:1–19—25–26

Leviticus

11:44–45—84
18—92
20—92

Numbers

22—24

Psalms

22—14–15
22:1—14
22:7—14
22:18—14
69—14–15
69:21—14

Isaiah

6:9–10—44

Jeremiah

31:15—15

Daniel

12:6–8—18

Hosea

11:1—15

Malachi

3:6—84

Matthew

2:14–15—15
2:16–18—15
4—72
5:8—52
10—28
10:29—28, 119
10:30—119
13:13–15—52
13:14–15—44
16:17—44
23:23—70
26:52—58
27:34—14
27:35—14
27:39—14
27:46—14
27:48—14

Mark

8:18—52

Luke

22:36—58

John

3:3—52
5:24—52
10:3—52, 119
11:49–52—15–16, 18
14–16—41
14:2–3—42
14:13–14—42
14:16–17—42
14:17—42
14:21—42
14:23—42
14:26—41
14:27—42
14:28—83
15:3–4—42
15:5—42
15:7—42
15:10—42
15:15—42
15:16—42
15:26—41
16:2—42
16:7–11—42
16:13—41
16:15—41
16:16—42
16:22—42
16:23—42
16:24—42
16:27—42
16:33—42

Acts

4:12—92, 94–95
17:11—40
26:4–23—35

Romans

1:21—44
1:25—44
2:5—44–45
10:17—52
11:8—45

1 Corinthians

2:13–14—34
2:14—34–35, 40
3:19—41
4:3—40
8:13—76

11:3–16—58
16:2—70

2 Corinthians

3:16—43
3:18—43
4:3–4—43
4:6—43, 44

Galatians

Book of—85

Ephesians

1:18—52

1 Thessalonians

4:15—63

Hebrews

6:18—84

1 Peter

1:10–12—15, 18

James

Book of—85
1:17—84

1 John

3:6—52

Revelation

6–8—29

Subject Index

Affirmation, 23, 31
Agnostics and interpretation, 36
Allegorization, 12, 34
Allen, Diogenes, 108
American Academy of Religion, 123
Analytical philosophy, 86–87
Anselm, 48
Application, 17, 25, 26: Hirschian, 16
Atheists and interpretation, 36
Augustine, 12, 81
Aulen, Gustaf, 80
Authorial intent: assessment of, 19–31; correctives to, 31–32; criticism of, 14–17; defense of, 18–19; nature of, 11–32

Barr, James, 89, 123
Beecher, Willis J., 18, 28–29
Biblical criticism: evaluation of, 90; and evangelicalism, 121–22
Biblical theology, 39, 41
Biblical Theology movement, 123
Big Bang theory, 108, 121
Blomberg, Craig L., 92–94
Bright, John, 67
Bultmann, Rudolf, 49

Calvinism, 105
Canonical interpretation, 18–19
Canonical theology, 84–85
Carson, D. A., 91n
Case study method, 117
Childs, Brevard, 84–85

Church history, hermeutical contributions of, 78–83
Commonsense notion: hard-core, 113–14; soft-core, 113
Communication, unconscious, 21, 23
Contemporization, 55–76: apparent contradictions and, 72–75; and evangelicalism, 56–57; identification of principles in, 65–72; isolation of time factor and, 64–65; issues involved in, 57–59; need for, 58–59; nondialogical approach to, 58; principlization and, 75–76; problem of, 55–57; significance and, 59–62; signification and, 59–62; three-step hermeneutics and, 62–64; two-step hermeneutics and, 62–64
Contextualization, temporal, 68, 73, 80–81
Contradictions, treatment of, 72–75
Copernican revolution, 22, 58
Cottonpatch Bible, The, 56
Cross-cultural studies, hermeneutical contributions of, 95–98
Culture-lag, evangelical, 104

Darwinism, 22, 109
Death of God, hermeutic of, 110
Deconstruction, 102, 104: hermeutic of, 110–13
Decontexualization, 69
Depravity, total, 44–45

Depth psychology, 21
Derridá, Jacques, 102, 110, 112
Descartes, René, 100, 106
Determinism, 106
Doctrine: as basis of timeless truth, 67, 84–85; cultural influences on, 80
Double meaning, 12, 29
Dynamic equivalence, 63–64, 65

Einstein, Albert, 115
Eisegesis, 85, 96, 97
Eliot, T. S., 13
Enthymemes, 92–94
Epistemology, biblical doctrine of, 51–52
Ethics, problem of, 68
Evangelicalism: and contemporization, 56–57; and culture-lag, 104; and postmodernism, 103–5; view of Scripture, 55
Exegesis: as believer, 36–37, 39, 43, 45, 47–51; versus exposition, 63; and illumination, 47; as unbeliever, 36–37, 38, 39, 43, 45, 47–51

Fletcher, Joseph, 65, 72–73
Flew, Antony, 31
Foundationalism, 102, 106–7, 114–16
Fourfold meaning of Scripture, 12
Freud, Sigmund, 21
Freudian slip, 21
Fuller, Daniel P., hermeneutical theory of, 33–54: analysis of, 37–39; basic tenets of, 33–37; evaluation of, 40–54

Gadamer, Hans Georg, 12
Generic prophecy, 18, 28–29
Gilkey, Langdon, 120
Glenn, Alfred A., 45–46
Globalism, 124–25
Goldingay, John, 65–66
Grammatical-historical meaning, 46, 49
Graves, Michael, 102
Griffin, David Ray, 102, 113–14

Hermeneutics: church history and, 78–83; cross-cultural studies and, 95–98; as exegesis, 101; individu-alistic approach to, 122–23; and linguistics, 123; multicultural approach to, 124–25; and naturalistic assumptions, 122; philosophical basis for, 123–24; postmodern, 114–25; postmodernism and, 99–125; theology and, 83–95; three-step, 64; two-step, 63
Hirsch, E. D., Jr., 11, 16, 59, 118: assessment of, 19–31
Historical conditioning, 81
Historical criticism, 101, 121
Historical relativism, 81
Historicism, new, 102
Holistic view of human nature, 46
Holy Spirit: as coauthor of Scripture, 31, 32; role in biblical interpretation, 31, 33–54
Hordern, William E., 57
Hume, David, 100, 106–7

Illumination, 33, 47: and exegesis, 51–54
Indeterminacy, Heisenberg's principle of, 108, 121
Inspiration, and the relationship between divine and human authors, 16
Inspiration of Scripture, 50: dynamic, 116–17; verbal, 116–17
Intention, 17, 18–19, 20–23: versus affirmation, 23, 31; versus assertion, 31; of biblical authors, 24; Hirschian, 21–22; and implication, 25–26, 31
Interpretation: aim of, 69; canonical process approach to, 18–19; and context, 91–92; of ethical material, 68–70; historical scholarship and, 67; historical limitations of, 81–82; historical variations of, 78–79; implications of, 83, 90, 94; intersubjectivity in, 54; role of Holy Spirit in, 33–54; of New Testament authors, 14–16, 29; presuppositions and, 81–82, 88–89, 95–96, 97; redaction criticism in, 74; subjectivism in, 12, 13–14, 30, 31, 54, 96;

suppressed premises and, 92–94; verification of, 89–90

James, William, 107, 115

Johnson, Alan, 57

Kaiser, Walter C., Jr., 11, 11n, 13–14, 17, 18–21, 23–25, 26, 28, 30, 74

Kant, Immanuel, 48

Kierkegaard, Søren, 100

Kraft, Charles, 63–64, 65

Language: concepts of, 116; of deconstruction, 110–12; predication and, 48; propositions and, 48; referents of, 116; religious, 52; representative-expressivist theory of, 107; Taylor's view of, 111–12

Lewis, C. S., 90

Living Bible, The, 56

Logical positivism, 86, 107, 118

Lundin, Roger, 104

Luther, Martin, 81

Lynch, David, 102

Mackintosh, C. H., 47

McKnight, Edgar V., 12

McQuilken, J. Robertson, 59, 65

Meaning, 19, 31, 59, 60, 61, 62, 101: Hirschian, 16, 22, 23, 59; inclusive understanding of, 20; versus meaningfulness, 117–18; modification of, 36–37; pragmatic dimension of, 60; and religious language, 52; semantic dimension of, 60; and significance, 23–26; as signification, 20, 26, 31–32; types of, 17, 26

Meaningfulness, 117–20

Metahermeneutics, 124

Metaphysics, process, 103

Mickelsen, A. Berkeley, 63

Miracles, 49

Modernism, 100–101: agreement with premodernism, 100–101; basic tenets of, 105–7; disagreement with premodernism, 100–101; erosion of, 107–10; historical criticism and, 101

Morris, Charles, 20n, 60

Multiculturalism, 124–25

Multiple fulfillments of prophecy, 10

Naturalism: first-level, 49; second-level, 50; third-level, 50

Needs, fundamental human, 119–20

Nelson, James, 91–92

Neopragmatism, 102

Nominalism, 84

Nondialogical approach to interpretation, 58

Origen, 33–34, 38, 47

Pannenberg, Wolfhart, 118

Pannenberg circle, 123

Payne, Philip B., 17

Pelagianism, epistemological, 45

Perspective, historical, 82

Perspectives, 123

Phenomenology, 120

Pinnock, Clark, 92, 94–95

Plato, 38

Platonism, 116

Positivism, logical, 118

Postmodernism: constructive, 103; critical evaluation of, 112–15; deconstructive, 102, 103–4, 110, 112–14; definition of, 101–3; and hermeneutics, 99–125; importance to evangelicalism, 103–5; liberationist, 103; restorationist, 102, 103

Pound, Ezra, 13

Poythress, Vern, 16–17, 26

Premodernism, 100–101: agreement with modernism, 100–101; disagreement with modernism, 100–101

Presuppositionalism, 115–16

Presuppositions, 30, 37, 39, 82, 88–89, 97

Principle of indeterminacy, 108, 121

Principlization, 23–24, 65n, 73–74: of the contemporary situation, 75–76; identification of principles in, 65–72; systematic theology in, 74

Prophecy: eschatological hermeneutic and, 12; fulfillment of, 14–15, 28–30; generic, 18, 28–29

Psychology, faculty, 45–46

Ramm, Bernard, 43–44, 52

Ramsey, Ian, 52, 54
Rationalism: epistemological, 107; theological, 39
Reader-response criticism, 12, 31
Realism, 84: metaphysical, 107
Reductionism, 106
Relativity, theory of, 115
Revelation, Pannenberg's theory of, 118–19
Riggs, Jack R., 15
Robinson, Haddon, 62, 67
Rorty, Richard, 102, 111

Schleiermacher, Friedrich, 100
Scientific method, 105
Scripture: contextualization of, 68; ethical statements in, 68; inspiration of, 116–17; paraphrastic translations of, 56–57; writing of, 50
Semiotic, 20n
Sensus plenior, Roman Catholic version of, 12, 30
Sermon: application, 27; and communication of biblical truth, 27–28; doctrinal principles in, 67–68; introduction, 26–27; possible topics of, 28, 86
Significance, 19, 20, 31–32, 48–49, 59, 61–62: Hirschian, 16, 19, 20, 59; and meaning, 23–26, 59; and relationship to principles, 24–25; versus signification, 117–20

Signification, 20, 26, 31–32, 48–49, 58–62, 64, 69–72
Sin: effects on biblical/theological truth, 87; effects on intellect, 38, 44–46; effects on will, 38, 44–46
Situation ethics, 65, 72–73
Smart, James, 63
Society of Biblical Literature, 123
Society of Christian Philosophers, 114
Stendahl, Krister, 36
Stipulative definition, 20
Summa theologiae, 86
Supernaturalism, versus naturalism, 49–50

Taylor, Mark, 110, 111–12, 114
Theology: analytical philosophy and, 86–87; hermeneutical contributions of, 83–95; problem of, 68–69
Thiselton, Anthony, 123–24
Thomas Aquinas, 86
Tiessen, Terrance, 66
Tigerman, Stanley, 102
Two horizons concept, 12
Translator-transformer distinction, 57
Truth: correspondence theory of, 107, 111; pragmatic theory of, 107
Typology, 15

Unconscious meaning, 22

Verification principle, 86–87

Waltke, Bruce K., 18